JCSS Study no. 22

Deterrence in the Middle East: Where Theory and Practice Converge

Aharon Klieman and Ariel Levite, Editors

WESTVIEW PRESS
Boulder • San Francisco • Oxford

THE JERUSALEM POST
Jerusalem

Publication of the Jaffee Center for Strategic Studies, Tel Aviv University

This Westview softcover edition is printed on acid-free paper and bound in library-quality, coated covers that carry the highest rating of the National Association of State Textbook Administrators, in consultation with the Association of American Publishers and the Book Manufacturers' Institute.

All rights reserved. No part of this publication may be reproduced or transmitted in any form or by any means, electronic or mechanical, including photocopy, recording, or any information storage and retrieval system, without permission in writing from the publisher.

Copyright © 1993 by Tel Aviv University, Jaffee Center for Strategic Studies

Published in 1993 in Israel by The Jerusalem Post, POB 81, Jerusalem 91000, Israel

Published in 1994 in the United States of America by Westview Press, Inc., 5500 Central Avenue, Boulder, Colorado 80301-2877, and in the United Kingdom by Westview Press, 36 Lonsdale Road, Summertown, Oxford OX2 7EW

CIP data available upon request
ISBN 0-8133-2220-0 (USA)

Printed and bound in the United States of America

∞ The paper used in this publication meets the requirements of the American National Standard for Permanence of Paper for Printed Library Materials Z39.48-1984.

10   9   8   7   6   5   4   3   2   1

Contents

		Page
Part I.		1
Chapter 1.	Introduction *Aharon Klieman*	3
Chapter 2.	Deterrence in an Israeli Security Context *Yitzhak Rabin*	6
Part II.	**The General Theory**	17
Chapter 3.	The Evolution of Deterrence Theory: Lessons for Israel *Barry Buzan*	19
Chapter 4.	Between General and Immediate Deterrence *Bruce Russett*	34
Chapter 5.	Asymmetrical Deterrence *Athanassios G. Platias*	45
Chapter 6.	The Limits of Deterrence Theory *George Downs*	63
Part III.	**Middle Eastern Application**	85
Chapter 7.	Arab Rationality and Deterrence *Gabriel Ben Dor*	87
Chapter 8.	Deterrence Experience in the Arab-Israel Conflict *Yair Evron*	98
Chapter 9.	Israeli Deterrence and the Gulf War *Shai Feldman*	122
Chapter 10.	Concluding Remarks: Reflections on Deterrence Beyond the Superpower Context *Ariel Levite*	149
Biographical Sketches of Contributors		163

Part I

1. Introduction

Aharon Klieman

Nowhere is it engraved in stone that all academic conferences merit being publicized, or must result in book publication. Certainly this was far from the minds of the directors of Tel Aviv University's Jaffee Center for Strategic Studies, and the co-sponsoring TAU Department of Political Science, when the decision was originally taken to host an international symposium in May 1991 on modern deterrence strategy. The intention was rather modest: to bring together a select group of scholars and theoreticians from abroad as well as Israel, and have them interact with local military planners and specialists in a relaxed atmosphere, akin to a workshop, to discuss specific aspects of deterrence thought.

During the proceedings, however, it soon became evident that the conference participants were saying something both original and of enduring, wider importance. A subsequent reading of the transcript and formal paper presentations reinforced our impression. Thus, upon undertaking this follow-up project the present coeditors had no hesitation in accepting what, indeed, has been a pleasant editing assignment.

Moreover, the added value of this book derives from the extraordinary, almost exquisite timing of the conference. Here, too, the scheduling, like the academic setting and format, had been governed solely by such apolitical considerations as the school year and university recesses. Yet by the time the meeting finally convened--as noted, in mid-1991--two system-transforming international events had converged to lend an air of far greater significance to the discussions on deterrence: on the one hand, the liberation by force of Kuwait; and on the other, the liberation (possibly only temporarily) of world politics from the balance of nuclear terror. As a result, what had begun as an unpretentious, theoretical seminar came to assume immediate and practical import.

Nor have international developments since then subtracted from the insights offered at the conference. We are confident the reader will find this collection of essays of abiding interest in the current post-Cold War, post-Gulf War setting. This, for several reasons. First, our authors remove a good deal of the mystery behind theories of deterrence. For all too long this entire specialized field has tended to be distant and off-limits--a subject possessing its own complex terminology and thus unintelligible to the outsider, to the uninitiated and to the nonexpert. This book has been crafted with the average layperson as much in mind as the specialist.

Secondly, the essays extend the concept of deterrence beyond the narrower confines of **nuclear** deterrence. As Friedrich von Gentz observed as early as 1806, "the fear of awakening common vengeance must of itself be sufficient to keep every one within the bounds of moderation." This is as good as any pre-atomic formulation of the essence of deterrence thinking in traditional diplomacy, military strategy, and interstate relations. It is also a timely reminder of conventional deterrence's continued logic and vitality, even as the emphasis perhaps shifts from the balance of terror to renewed balance-of-power politics. Deterrence will surely remain a permanent feature, indeed a central pillar, in both eventualities.

Third, the book draws attention not only to the superpower and European arenas which have preoccupied deterrence literature for over 40 years, but also to non-superpower confrontational situations that now dominate and threaten along the periphery, and in the Middle East in particular. Can the calculus of deterrence be said to function as compellingly among small powers as among great ones? Will Arabs and Israelis essentially replicate the rules of deterrence engagement adopted in the bipolar East-West struggle, or are they more likely to develop an original set of their own? In either event, Middle East deterrence models in a world of uncertainty are guaranteed to make their distinctive contribution--inspirational or otherwise--to our understanding of deterrence's two dimensions: its theoretical assumptions, but also its mechanics when applied to real world situations in the 1990s.

One notes of late a growing advocacy for delegitimizing, undermining or even dismantling the entire strategy of deterrence as a small price of admission into a new world order. Begging to differ, the editors and the Jaffee Center offer this volume. These revised and updated conference proceedings have been prepared in the spirit of realistically adapting and universalizing classic as well as nuclear deterrence frameworks to the new regional and global conditions--conditions that challenge not only Israel but all members of an ever-vigilant, rearming and security-conscious international community.

2. Deterrence in an Israeli Security Context

Yitzhak Rabin

[this lecture was delivered in May 1991, when Mr. Rabin held no governmental office]

In this presentation of deterrence as a component of ongoing Israeli security, I will express ideas and conceptions based upon my experience as chief of staff, prime minister, and minister of defense.

One must first define the two levels of threat to Israel's security. The first is to the very existence of the state, a threat that can be carried out only by the armed forces of the Arab countries led by radical, hostile leaders--Saddam Hussein of Iraq for example, or Hafez al-Asad of Syria--or those who may yet appear in the future. This is the principal threat to Israel, and it is not by sheer coincidence that some 90 percent of the annual defense budget appropriation goes to building capabilities for coping with strategic threat at this level of magnitude.

The second level, however, is aimed against the security of individual Israelis anywhere, especially in particularly vulnerable areas. This threat can be carried out by terror, Palestinian or Shi'ite, from beyond the borders or within. The latter, referred to as the Palestinian civilian uprising or intifada, is a relatively new phenomenon (since 1987) in the West Bank and Gaza. But because they do not endanger the very existence of the State, these second-level threats cannot be compared to the first. Each must be dealt with differently and in its own specific context.

Let us not forget that terror has been, is and will be the weapon of the weak. Therefore, with regard to the intifada, for all practical purposes I do not believe that one can construct a fool-proof deterrent against it. Whether terror comes from the outside or from within, as in the intifada, measures can be effective in reducing or eliminating it for limited periods only. Consequently, strictly speaking, in discussing deterrence strategies we ought to limit ourselves to the principal threat to the very physical existence of Israel by conventional military forces unleashed by one or more Arab countries.

Since the mid-'50s, the first question troubling formulators of defense policy in Israel has been whether our military strength can be employed in keeping with three axioms of war: (1) that force be an extension of policy by other means; (2) that when in conflict the aim is to destroy both the enemy's forces and its will to continue fighting; (3) that the original political objectives which made war necessary be achieved when the fighting terminates. We constantly ask ourselves: Within the very specific parameters of the Arab-Israel conflict, is it possible for the Israeli army to achieve what the Allied forces were able to accomplish in World War II against the Axis? Or, put differently, is it possible to achieve unconditional surrender with the intention of imposing a political goal, thereby eliminating in the long run both our adversary's desire and his material prospects for resuming hostilities against us? I believed in the mid-'50s, as I believe today, that what happened in 1945 in Europe and the Pacific-- the capture of Rome or Berlin, releasing A-bombs on Hiroshima and Nagasaki, the imposition of political and social reforms on Germany (including the division of Germany into two Germanies), Italy and Japan--is simply unthinkable for Israel, as well as impossible in terms of the Middle East.

In our case, between Arab forces, Israeli forces and "the one who reigns in Heaven," there are the intervening Great Powers. And whether acting individually or in concert, they have exercised considerable influence each time Middle East war has erupted. Moreover, if this was true in the past, I believe today we are reaching a point in world politics when even if, for the sake of argument, Israel were to channel all its resources into defense, somehow capture Arab capitals, and then be positioned to occupy indefinitely all the neighboring Arab countries and impose on them the kind of reforms needed to eliminate any further motivation for war against Israel--it is absolutely inconceivable that such a scenario and goal could be implemented. Hence, is it possible for Israel to initiate "a war to end all wars," and to impose peace on the Arab countries? My unequivocal answer to this first question is that such a possibility is totally nonexistent. As a result, there is no valid purpose for Israel deliberately to initiate war against an Arab country or Arab countries if the intention is to achieve an ultimate political solution through the forced imposition of peace.

Twice we tried and failed to achieve such a goal. In 1956, in collaboration with Britain and France, the goal was to eliminate Gamal Abdul Nasser's regime and, hopefully, for Israel to gain control of Sinai. The second failure occurred in 1982 when we operated alone in Lebanon, going so far as to sign a dubious "peace treaty" on May 17, 1983 between the so-called government of Lebanon and the Government of Israel. This non-binding document was not worth the price of the paper on which it was signed even before the ink of the signatures dried. Yet it has at least reconfirmed the futility of attempting to use military power on behalf of far-reaching political goals.

Having thus eliminated any argument for Israel's deliberately launching a war for peace, let us now consider if there might be other logical reasons for Israel, nevertheless, to consider precipitating war.

There have always been leaders and countries, like Saddam Hussein and Iraq in the two recent Persian Gulf wars, that have set territorial expansion as a goal. I personally do not believe, nor do I know of any government in Israeli history that has considered it to be in Israel's vital interest to initiate a war solely in order to acquire additional territory. In my humble opinion, we have more territories than we require or know what to do with. Therefore I exclude this goal, too.

A third possibility is a deliberate preemptive war to destroy the enemy's military potential, for fear that within a year or less those armed forces could reach a point of offensive fighting effectiveness at which they would enjoy the option of a conventional first strike. I do not believe that such a goal justifies initiation of war, if only because future wars will be neither swift nor easy, and surely not painless for a small state like Israel.

After all, we know that in the case of the Arab countries, there is little point in striking major strategic targets in order to eliminate the capability of the Arab countries to produce arms, since their major sources of arms are external. And if we have learned anything from all our past wars, it is that after each round of fighting more and better military hardware was shipped to the Arab countries, and more quickly than any of us believed possible.

Because I can see no justification--political, territorial or military--for implementing a policy of deliberate and prepared war, we are left with the conclusion that the best policy for Israel is to prevent wars from occurring in the 1990s.

The more time that passes without war, the better it is for Israel. Moreover, the longer Israel is successful in deterring an Arab leader or coalition from being tempted to initiate war, the better become the longer-term prospects for peace. Basically, the precondition for peace is the other side's realization that it cannot gain from Israel through the use of violence--war or terror--more than is obtainable from negotiations.

When I was minister of defense, I considered the major test of Israel's defense policy its ability to prevent hostilities by verbal deterrence. No Arab hesitates to go to war because of the color of our eyes or noble moral principles; an opponent has to bear in mind only one imperative: the risks it incurs in going to war against us.

What, then, is needed (and I limit myself now to conventional warfare between the Arab states and Israel) to deter a leader like Hafez al-Asad from going to war? If he thought Israel's capability of responding to his attack lay only in preventing him from achieving his goals, there would have been ceaseless war between Syria and Israel during the past 15 years. If the worst an Arab leader can perceive as happening as a result of a war he initiates is that he will not achieve his goal, then this is insufficient deterrence on Israel's part. Rather, an Arab leader like Asad must constantly bear in mind that, should he initiate war, his armed forces will be badly clobbered, along with sensitive targets causing disruption to the local population, and in a way that will endanger his regime. Otherwise, our deterrence will be minimal.

At this point, one might rightly ask whether there is any political role left for military power. Answering in the affirmative, I am convinced that by a combination of deterrence and, should deterrence fail, a decisive battlefield victory, the function of the IDF is to compel the Arabs to shift the quest for a solution of the Arab-Israel conflict from the battlefield to the negotiating table, and to Israel's great advantage. Proof lies in the post-Yom Kippur War period. President Sadat's realization that he could claim to have satisfied Egyptian dignity and also secure tangible benefits from the fighting as it ended at kilometer 101, led him to shift from military confrontation to diplomatic negotiation.

What kind of army is required by Israel at present to fulfill this formulation of deterrence? To be explicit: armed forces with the greatest offensive potential. For if attacked, we must be able immediately to transfer the war to enemy territory, to destroy as much of the aggressor's armed forces as possible, and to pose a credible strategic threat to that country's very regime.

In our circumstances, this means offensive-type armed forces: strike helicopters, mobile units, paratroopers, missiles and a deep-penetration air force, as well as all of the requisite backup electronic and intelligence systems.

Again, the basic strategy of Israel is defensive, to prevent war, to deter from war. Yet, ironically, the best means for preserving the status quo is by possessing this ultimate offensive capability in reserve--and at a high state of military preparedness. I am talking, to be sure, only about conventional forces. Therefore, I see no contradiction in designing the armed forces of Israel for this dual purpose: deterrence and, if deterrence fails, achievement of a quick, decisive victory.

In addition, there is the question of our entire philosophy and national mentality, or "mindset," that indirectly affects Israeli notions of deterrence. When I visited the United States after the Gulf War, people sought to point out to me that American casualties against sizeable Iraqi armed forces had been minimal; less, in fact, than ours were in any one of the Arab-Israeli wars. I had to explain the basic difference between the United States fighting Iraq, and Israel fighting its wars in the past and, if we have to, even in the future.

The United States enjoyed, both politically and logistically, a long breathing space in preparing its riposte. Even after the actual fighting commenced, no one would have dared tell the Americans after the sixth or eighteenth or twenty-first day: "Stop fighting." We know, on the other hand, that our time is limited. Whatever is not won within a relatively short period--hours or at most days--endangers our prospects for achieving the purpose of our wars, even when they are forced upon us. Secondly, of course, we have no comparable logistical respite simply because of our limited human, financial and material resources. We have always paid dearly in blood and loss of materiel for this quantitative deficiency.

I will make only one further comparison. The US Air Force and its allies numbered 1,200 fighters and bombers deployed in the Gulf War. Of these, about 40 planes were lost in combat, or three per 100. During the 1967 Six-Day War, we lost 12 percent of our fighters in combat in six days, that is, 24 out of 200 planes. During the 1973 Yom Kippur War we lost almost one-third of our air force; out of slightly over 300 planes in our arsenal at that time, 100 fighters were downed in 18 days.

These statistics derive from entirely different approaches, methods and tactics used by the IAF and the US Air Force. They have time; we do not. This alone dictates our designing a more effective preventive or deterring posture; also one with greater prospects for winning decisively and as quickly as possible.

I see no reason to change our basic thinking or attitude, notwithstanding the heavy and painful cost of this strategy. When I was minister of defense, some of our leading military people asked: What is the definition of Israel winning a war? Is it taking an Arab capital? Is it overrunning certain territories? I defined it quite simply, as follows: winning is when the attacking country or countries ask for a ceasefire, or merely cease firing on the spot. To date, the Arab armies have not succeeded in wresting any bit of Israel's own land, whereas we have acquired territories that can strategically threaten their regimes. For me, this in itself constitutes a victory; and it cannot be measured only according to the sheer number of enemy planes, tanks or soldiers eliminated. Instead, victory is mirrored by the overall political, military, geographic and even psychological situation.

In reviewing to what extent the Israeli deterrence doctrine has worked, in the narrow sense of dissuading an Arab state or coalition of states from initiating war against Israel, I cannot claim it has succeeded throughout Israel's existence. For if so, there would not have been any wars. We must therefore take into account that deterrence in conventional warfare in the Middle East is not foolproof. Consequently, when formulating our overall defense policy and its purpose, we must consider deterrence effective if there is credibility in our political preparedness and in our military combat readiness, once we are attacked, to go to war in the most decisive and speedy manner.

I believe that since Egypt opted out of the ruinous war cycle by signing the 1979 peace treaty, Israel's deterrence capability has functioned even more effectively. There has been no initiation of war against Israel by any Arab state in the context of the Arab-Israel conflict. What happened in 1982 in Lebanon was initiated by Israel, not Syria. If at all, it came about because of terrorist activities by PLO groups from Lebanese territory which the Beirut authorities were incapable of preventing.

I also know that in the wake of the Gulf Crisis, the use of force by the United States and its allies, and the Scuds launched against Israel, some people believe Israel's policy of restraint damaged its deterrence capability. I do not in any way buy this argument.

First, Israel's deterrent capability must be measured: (a) only in the narrow framework of the Arab-Israel conflict, and (b) by the extent a neighboring Arab state chooses all-out war against Israel. Secondly, because I happen to believe the surface-to-surface missile threat from Syria to be far greater than from Iraq, as minister of defense I believed it our duty to make it clear that any attempt to launch conventional missiles on Tel Aviv would be returned a hundred-fold on Damascus and other Syrian cities. I made this warning public, bearing in mind the possibility of Scud missiles aimed at us mainly from Syria. And I know the message reached Damascus loud and clear, and was taken seriously.

The challenge embodied in the threat of conventional missiles is not primarily to locate, hit, or intercept them. It is to deter their being employed in the first place. And the only way to do this is by declaring in advance that Damascus will suffer three times more destruction than Tel Aviv--by retaliatory means that do not even need to be elaborated.

In the case of the 1991 Gulf Crisis, once preponderant multinational force was initiated against Iraq, Israel's capabilities became almost irrelevant in the Iraqi equation simply because Saddam was facing the overwhelming combined military power of the United States and its allies. Besides, the Iraqi leader knew Israel could not, would not, and need not respond by bombing Baghdad on a large scale. Therefore in that truly singular instance, Israel's deterrence capability could not be fully evaluated because fear of an Israeli reaction did not in itself suffice to deter the firing of a few missiles.

If anything, I am convinced our deterrent capability has increased as a result of the crisis in the Gulf, if only indirectly and because the United States demonstrated its readiness to act resolutely. I am not saying that Washington will automatically do the same for Israel; nor has Israel ever asked the United States to do so. But the fact that this time the United States stood firm and was ready to become involved against an aggressor in the Middle East, adds somewhat to Israel's overall deterrence. It discourages initiation of war in the region, though I do not know for how long.

There is a corollary that applies to weapons of mass destruction, and particularly to the chemical warfare threat. We ought to have made an authoritative declaration drawing a clear-cut line between conventional Scuds and those carrying chemical warheads. We ought to have stated that: "Even in the context of the Gulf War, any use of mass destruction weapons against the citizens and the civilian population of Israel will be met by comparable weapons against Baghdad with or without American consent." Nor would Israel have had to specify what weapons would be used. As a Jewish state, Israel cannot tolerate the use of poison gas against Jews a second time in this century.

I believe this is the "red line" Israel ought to have made explicit from the very beginning of the 1990-1991 crisis. Should there be a next time, Israel cannot and will not tolerate the use of ballistic or chemical warfare without responding forcefully against Baghdad and other Iraqi targets. I am not saying exactly what the response should be. I certainly do not believe it should be deliberated in public or unnecessarily elaborated upon.

I am convinced that deterrent capability is possible even vis-a-vis conventional Scuds. Basically, Arab military commanders of late have come to believe in push-button weapons. Once having managed to cope with air defense by using surface-to-air missiles, they would like to reach the heart of Israel by surface-to-surface missiles, rather than rely exclusively on pilots for either aerial defense or for offensive air penetration. With regard to the nonconventional end of the spectrum, I have already noted in terms of the chemical warfare threat why there must be a clear-cut policy that Israel will not tolerate any use of weapons of mass destruction, beginning even with the simplest chemical ones. Let us hope there will not be anything beyond that.

I know many people ask, "Who says that Arab leaders are rational?", and then proceed to answer themselves by insisting, "They are not logical." Consider, however: Saddam Hussein may have been a megalomaniac, but he was not crazy. True, he miscalculated, and on a grand scale: first, when he did not appreciate that the US would stand firm. Secondly, I believe he was prepared to suffer casualties in Kuwait, and to endure war, but like most analysts, he did not expect the air strikes to continue more than two-three weeks, whereas they lasted for almost five weeks before the ground fighting began. And of course, he made a major mistake obvious to anyone who has experienced war with the Arab states. About eight days before the fighting started, he sent Tariq Aziz to Moscow with the revolutionary council's decision, also announced by the communications media of Iraq, that he was ready to yield Kuwait. I do not know of any soldier in the Arab world who is ready to fight for something his own leaders have conceded in advance.

To return to our main topic: Even though no deterrence is foolproof in the context of conventional warfare between the Arab states and Israel, deterrence capability is vital for Israel in preventing wars. We might win; but, still, any future war will not only be costly, but in all probability will lead nowhere politically or diplomatically. If this is the case, why should we not continue trying our best to avoid such senseless confrontations by investing in defensive capability? Especially since building this capability does not offset, but rather complements those categories of military forces necessary for winning once war has been forced on us.

In sum, I believe that Israel's deterrent capabilities have been effective thus far. They have proved themselves during the last two decades, including the Gulf War. For the fact is that Saddam Hussein did not initiate war against Israel, but rather against the weaker party, Kuwait.

Part II

The General Theory

3. The Evolution of Deterrence Theory: Lessons for Israel

Barry Buzan

My subject is the evolution of deterrence theory, and the theme here is "theory and practice." I am not entirely convinced that this distinction between theory and practice is an easy one to follow, because the theory and practice of deterrence have always been very closely intertwined. Indeed, it might be argued that they have been so closely intertwined that it has been difficult to tell the difference. This means, in effect, that the evolution of what we think of as deterrence theory has been very closely tied to the evolution of policy, particularly American policy.

It has therefore also been tied to the particular circumstances of American policymaking, the rivalry with the Soviet Union, the evolution of nuclear technology, and so on. These things cannot be disentangled.

I take it also that the purpose of this exercise is not simply to present the evolution of deterrence theory in and of itself, but to establish in some way its relevance for the particular problems of Israel. This poses some difficulties because, obviously, the circumstances of Israel are quite different from the circumstances of the United States. What I will try to do therefore, is to present a fairly simple or, if you will, oversimplified sketch of how deterrence theory has unfolded historically. I will do this in part simply by giving a short intellectual history, and in part by trying to touch on a number of themes, looking in particular at the way that technology has driven the evolution of deterrence theory, and the way in which various situational factors have also impinged upon the development of this theory.

By following this line, I hope to be able to specify some of the points at which the evolution of deterrence theory seems to have significance for the situation of Israel, and some of the areas in which it does not. Thus I will try not only to sketch, as it were, the history, but also to establish an agenda of relevance.

To begin with, one of the striking differences is that deterrence theory developed in a relationship between superpowers geographically remote from each other. That already establishes considerable disparity between the conditions for deterrence faced by the originators of deterrence theory, and the sorts of problems that you confront here.

One needs to bear this in mind. Deterrence theory is not a neat, detached body of theory that can simply be taken and applied anywhere directly, but it has developed essentially in the light of a particular policy problem, namely that faced by the United States, and in the light of a particular technology, namely the technology of nuclear weapons.

Now there is a fair measure of agreement about how to structure the intellectual history of deterrence theory. Most people speak in terms of three or possibly four waves or periods. Let me start by simply summarizing roughly what they are and how things developed during them.

What is usually referred to as the first wave, and this periodization comes from Colin Grey, was the really rather small group of people, mostly American and British, who responded in the 1940s and early 1950s to the development of nuclear weapons. There is a small body of works from this period which basically asked: "Well, what are the military implications of nuclear weapons? How do we deal with this new destructive force?"

During this period, many of the basic ideas of what we now think of as deterrence theory were worked out by people like Bernard Brodie, especially the notion that one had to shift toward a war-prevention strategy in order to deal with a military technology that had such a high level of destructiveness.

Some thought was also given to what would happen when more than one country acquired nuclear weapons. But the circumstances during this first period of deterrence theorizing were such that this effort had a relatively low profile. Deterrence theory was not something that would have motivated a seminar. It was not a matter of great public concern.

The reason for that, of course, was that only the United States had nuclear weapons, and therefore there was not that sense of urgency arising from a situation in which two parties armed with nuclear weapons confront each other.

So the first wave was a fairly quiet affair, although intellectually much of the basic foundation of later deterrence thinking was laid.

The second wave is usually referred to as the Golden Age. I am not quite sure why; nonetheless, this is an established terminology, and one cannot do anything about that! It began really around the middle of the 1950s and went through into the 1960s, petering out by the mid-1970s.

It began with a critique mounted on American policy which, at that time, called for massive retaliation: the Dulles/Eisenhower policy. Massive retaliation as a policy reflected the fact that the United States was the only country possessing nuclear weapons in significant quantities. There was therefore a unipolar construction in terms of nuclear power and, in this sense, the United States had a great deal of latitude in how it thought about using nuclear weapons.

But by the mid-1950s it was clear that this situation of American predominance was not going to last. The Soviet Union and others had already tested weapons and were quite clearly going to be in the game within a relatively few years. This created a much higher profile for theorizing about deterrence, and perhaps this is the explanation for the idea of the Golden Age. Simply, deterrence theory suddenly became popular, and you could get a lot of attention by talking about it. There was now a real problem to be dealt with. How was one to deploy nuclear weapons? How was one to think about using them in a situation wherein you faced an opponent also equipped with nuclear weapons, and therefore able to damage you as much as you could damage him?

The key thinking that emerged at this time, and became, as it were, an established wisdom, was that which related to mutual deterrence, deterrence between two parties, each standing the other off with threats of nuclear devastation. The central element that emerged here was the idea of mutual assured destruction, or MAD, that delightful acronym which has characterized many of the more satirical views of deterrence theories for a long period.

MAD theory was basically designed to create stability in a situation where both sides had the ability to inflict massive destruction on each other. It was neat, simple, rather pure logic. This may also be a reason for the term the Golden Age. Those were the days in which nuclear deterrence seemed relatively simple. It seemed like an idea that might easily reach the kind of intellectual closure in which everything meaningful that could be said had been said; here was a nice, basic idea which, if followed through in policy terms, could produce a useful kind of stability in what otherwise seemed a dangerous world.

The difficulty with this, and it is a difficulty that I will return to, emerged because of the particular problem that the United States faced of extended deterrence. By extended deterrence I mean that the Americans had made significant and substantial commitments to defend Western Europe against a potential Soviet attack. This meant that there was another angle to the unfolding game of deterrence. It was not just a matter of the United States and the Soviet Union standing each other off, but the Americans also had to be able to deter Soviet attacks on their allies.

This created very considerable logical difficulties. I have described this elsewhere as the worm in the apple of the Golden Age theory. For a time it seemed manageable; but as the problem of extended deterrence unfolded, it began more and more to undermine the simple and neat assumptions of mutually assured destruction.

The central problem of how to handle extended deterrence was that if the Americans used their deterrence threats to defend Europe, then all kinds of problems of credibility arose. These were summarized in the question of whether the Americans would sacrifice Washington for Hamburg. In other words, if the Russians attacked Western Europe, would the United States retaliate against the Soviet Union, knowing that the Soviet Union could still retaliate against the United States? If the answer to that question was no, or even that there would be great hesitations about it, then extended deterrence was in trouble.

So the policy problem that arose was that the Americans had committed themselves to an extended deterrence policy in relation to Europe at a time when doing so was easy, because they had the whip hand: they were the only country possessing nuclear weapons. But they had to continue this policy into a period in which the Soviets also had nuclear weapons, and in which, therefore, these guarantees became much more difficult to render believable.

This problem, the problem of extended deterrence, as I suggested, grew worse, and steadily undermined the credibility of mutually assured destruction. One of the nice things about mutual assured destruction was that it seemed possible to have such a policy with a fairly small number of nuclear weapons, and therefore to limit the force levels required.

Mutually assured destruction, in its pure form, did not necessarily seem to lead to open-ended arms racing, because you only needed a certain amount of power to completely destroy your opponent. You did not need more than that, and therefore there was, in some sense, an absolute ceiling of military capability required, and it was hoped that this would somehow cap arms racing tendencies.

Solving the problem of extended deterrence, however, steadily undermined this whole idea of minimum nuclear deterrence, and steadily increased the kind of force requirements that seemed necessary to make deterrence work, given the kinds of commitments that the United States had made. This dilemma led to what is referred to as the third wave, beginning in the mid-1970s. In this wave one gets a much more complicated view of deterrence, based not so much on the idea of retaliation as mutually assured destruction had been, but increasingly moving toward what are referred to as war-fighting policy, policies of denial, i.e., carefully staged patterns of response that would look like a controlled war, controlled escalation. One would not respond to an attack with all-out retaliation. One would respond in some way proportionately, trying to create a steadily graded level of responses which, it was hoped, would deter the Soviet Union.

This, curiously, created a kind of convergence between American and Soviet thinking about deterrence, but a convergence that was opposite to the one that had been expected. During the

Golden Age, many had assumed that the Golden Age theory was somehow absolutely right, and that it was only a matter of time before the Soviets would begin appreciating its wisdom.

The Soviets had always taken a more war-fighting view of deterrence: that you deterred by preparing to fight and win whatever conceivable war you might be confronting. Steadily, the United States was pushed more toward this Soviet-type view, and therefore more toward open-ended military preparations, and ever increasing force requirements in order to meet all of the requisites of escalation and escalation control within every possible type of escalation scenario.

The third wave, then, still rested on the logic of mutually assured destruction, but the difficulty of dealing with extended deterrence meant that the great simplicities of mutually assured destruction were buried under the mountains of complexities and scenarios necessary to deal with all of the possible problems that would arise in maintaining extended deterrence. It tended to generate much more open-ended military competition because, rather than simply requiring some absolute amount of force in order to punish your opponent, you needed the ability to fight at different levels and at different intensities, and therefore there was no obvious ceiling on the military requirements for pursuing this policy.

This third wave, which had risen in the mid-1970s, began to give way in the mid-1980s to what might be called a fourth wave, although here, as always when coming into the present, it becomes difficult to characterize matters in any coherent way.

One of the responses that might characterize the fourth wave was despair. There is a useful quote from Gregg Herken, which describes this quite well. He says, "Not since Brody's proclamation that strategy had hit a dead end had such profound doubt and despair accompanied the subject of nuclear weapons, nor such an apparently fundamental loss of faith in deterrence. The concept of mutually assured destruction has found few champions recently, but the confounders of MAD, the war-fighters, have thus offered no better hope than the tenuous and untested chance that a nuclear war might prove limited and controllable."

In other words, what had happened by the mid-1980s was that the logic of the third wave had worked itself out to a point of despair. It seemed that the logic of limited nuclear war, which implied highly rational, highly controlled behavior, was increasingly untenable. Nobody believed that you could control a limited nuclear war. Nobody believed that escalation control would really work. Or at least those who did believe it were not able to persuade the general masses that their line of logic was plausible.

So a situation was reached in which the Golden Age theory did not look very good, because it was far too simple and did not fit the complex circumstances of extended deterrence. But neither did the third wave war-fighting theory, for its part, look very impressive, because it seemed logically implausible, potentially dangerous and, whatever else, led to open-ended arms racing.

Two sorts of escape from this dilemma presented themselves. The first to emerge was the idea that a particular player could escape from the deterrence problem altogether by resorting to strategic defense technologies. If that player could reestablish the ability to defend himself and actually block or deny nuclear strikes, then he would avoid all of these awful logical dilemmas of deterrence and get back to something resembling more normal defense relations.

That logic, of course, was very strong during the Reagan administration. It had a big impact on thinking about deterrence, particularly in the United States.

A second route of escape was simply to take the view that all of these logical complexities did not matter, that at the end of the day there was a kind of existential deterrence, as it was referred to, whereby nuclear weapons were so appalling and so terrifying that no matter what the logical complexities, anybody facing the prospect of a nuclear war would be deterred. Existential deterrence was an act of great faith in the efficacy of pure terror.

A third line of escape has emerged more recently, one that has not yet been much explored, but which will be a happy line of release for some from these dilemmas. This is simply to say that deterrence theory is now irrelevant, that the Cold War is over, and therefore, everything that deterrence theory was constructed to meet no longer pertains. There is no longer a great threat or even a sense of hostility, and therefore, we do not have to worry about this very much. Especially since we have more to worry about in terms of economics and the like.

This, of course, is not of much comfort to countries like Israel, where, in effect, the Cold War is not over.

That, in broad brush terms is the intellectual history of deterrence as I see it.

Let me now go back and view it again, but in terms of more specific themes.

To start with, I would like to look at a technological theme-- at the things that drove the development of deterrence theory, and shaped it into the pattern that I have described.

The first technological driver was clearly nuclear weapons themselves, the availability of weapons of mass destruction and long-range vehicles by which they could be delivered to the enemy. This created a possibility of massive retaliation. You did not necessarily have to block your opponent's military attack; you could simply make it extremely expensive by inflicting punishment on him on his home ground.

This breakthrough was, in my view, very strongly dependent on nuclear weapons. There has been, of course, a logic of conventional deterrence which preceded the nuclear era and which has, in some senses, continued on through the nuclear era. Arguments about conventional deterrence were very much part of the third wave that I have described. But the general feeling--I think it fair to say--is that deterrence logic does not work very well with conventional weapons, because there is always the possibility that your opponent will take the risk. Again and again one sees that conventional deterrence, even at fairly high levels, has often neither prevented the outbreak of war nor stopped it. In this sense the key to deterrence was really the enormous destructiveness of nuclear weapons, which simply put beyond any doubt whatsoever that there could be a meaningful distinction between victory and defeat. And if you cannot make a distinction between victory and defeat, then there is no point in fighting.

So nuclear weapons and their mass destructiveness were crucial to the logic of deterrence. They were the first impetus in deterrence theory development. And, of course, this is a situation which--if we take as given that Israel has nuclear weapons--applies very strongly to the Israeli case.

The second technological driver came about as a result of improvements in delivery systems, whereby more accurate missiles, and also more missiles, opened up the possibility of disarming first strikes. That meant that one side could quite possibly eliminate the nuclear capabilities of the other in an all-out first strike.

This had two possible consequences. One was that if you were in a position to deliver a first strike, then you could escape from mutually assured destruction and all of its discomforts by eliminating your opponent's capability. On the other hand, however, looking at this in reverse, it meant that the threat of mutually assured destruction was also itself under threat, if only because it implied that one might find himself the victim of a first strike rather than its initiator.

That introduced a whole new level of insecurity into the deterrence game, and led to a tremendous effort to preserve what was called secure second strike forces. In other words, it led to a great technological effort, and also a considerable theoretical effort--part of the unfolding of Golden Age and third wave theory--to work out how to preserve your second strike forces against all possible contingencies.

This difficulty again undermined mutually assured destruction by increasing force level requirements. (I take it that so far, given Israeli air superiority, this particular dilemma has not yet arisen here, although it seems to be impending, given the spread of missile technology in the region.) And this move was, in a sense, one of the great drivers of deterrence theorizing because it made life much more complicated. A shift into a situation where mutual first strikes were possible is much less stable, much more angst-ridden than one in which this is not the case.

That technological problem drove deterrence theory all through the '60s, '70s and '80s, and led to very expensive technological attempts to address the problem. Partly in response to the apparently endless difficulty of maintaining a secure second strike against increasingly accurate strike forces, the logic of strategic defense emerged, as I have mentioned, during the 1980s.

This again was technologically driven--the possibility that one could actually stop a nuclear attack by intercepting it at various levels. This also offered, as I have suggested, an escape from MAD, an escape from all of the dilemmas of living in the uncomfortable world of mutual deterrence. It had also the possibility of restoring offensive options, of restoring, if you like, a situation of one-sided nuclear power, like the situation that the United States had enjoyed during the 1940s and the early part of the 1950s. If only one side had strategic defense, then that side could restore its nuclear strike options against its opponents.

If this is technologically feasible, then it would be extremely attractive to Israel in policy terms--but not in budgetary terms, simply because this becomes a very expensive line to pursue. In technological terms, however, one can see the nuclear evolution creating both loss and gain of options. Originally, nuclear weapons caused a loss of ability to defend one's self, but a gain in ability to retaliate. Deterrence logic was largely based on this ability to retaliate, but the possibility of strategic defense may mean that one loses the ability to retaliate if one's opponent has strategic defense.

One lesson from this, looking at technology as a driving force, is that any kind of technological advantage is unsustainable. There is, in a sense, a treadmill here. Consequently, whatever a new technology provides in the way of short-term advantage, will not be sustainable, for there is an endless dialogue or dialectic in the technology process that continuously changes the circumstances under which deterrence has to be pursued.

Let me now move away from technology and toward more situational factors that have also played a significant role in the evolution of deterrence theory.

One of these, polarity, has been referred to already: How many countries have nuclear weapons? When nuclear weapons were possessed by the United States alone, deterrence theory was relatively easy. The Americans could threaten others, while others could not threaten them.

It was the shift therefore, from unipolarity (a single country possessing nuclear weapons) to bipolarity (two countries possessing nuclear weapons), that was the major driver for deterrence theory. Deterrence theory, if you like, was designed to deal with the problem of two countries threatening each other mutually.

One of the difficulties raised by bipolarity was that the "threshold" of deterrence might rise. In other words, if two countries were threatening each other with nuclear weapons, it could well be that those threats would become mutually paralyzing, and they could open the way for conventional warfare between them. The image here is World War II, in which both sides were equipped with an array of very nasty poisonous gases and other chemical weapons, but did not use them, even though one side eventually went down to total defeat.

The possibility was therefore that nuclear deterrence would work in the sense that nuclear weapons would deter each other, but that they would not deter other types of war. Because of nuclear terror, the threshold of deterrence would rise to a point where other types of warfare might well become possible.

This, it seems to me, is a situation of considerable relevance to the Israeli case, in the sense that Israel has been in the unipolar position in its region for some time. But if it ceases to occupy that privileged position and faces local rivals similarly equipped, then all of the same kinds of logic that have unfolded from mutual deterrence and the difficulty of raised thresholds will also unfold.

These are very unattractive categories of logic. They are very expensive in terms of the military capabilities required, and they leave you facing logics of limited nuclear war, or limited war of one sort or another which are clearly completely unacceptable for a country of Israel's size.

So the shift from unipolar to bipolar very much emphasizes the interdependence aspect of deterrence, that the security of one state becomes very strongly dependent upon the behavior of another.

There is a third possible element here, the shift from bipolarity to multipolarity. This might become of general interest but, it seems to me, is not particularly relevant to the case of Israel.

I have already mentioned extended deterrence. This is a second situational factor that very strongly drove the evolution of deterrence theory. As I have suggested, it created an enormous problem for the United States: how to reinforce its deterrence guarantees for its European allies under conditions whereby the Americans themselves were threatened by the Soviet Union.

This essentially was what wrecked the simplicities of the Golden Age deterrence theory. It created a general divide in perceptions of deterrence which I have labeled "the Easy School" and "the Difficult School." The Easy School thinks that basically deterrence is fairly simple to arrange, that all you have to do is to be able to threaten your opponent with unacceptable destruction, and that this is the essential condition of deterrence, even if your threats are not very plausible. Even a five percent probability of inflicting nuclear destruction on somebody can achieve deterrence, because the level of destruction is so high.

The Difficult School is more associated with the logic of the third wave, and the attempt to respond to the difficulties of extended deterrence. It stresses the need not only for high destructive capabilities, but also for very high probabilities that these forces would be used.

Deterrence, in this view, is much more difficult to achieve. It requires much higher levels of force, much higher levels of credibility.

It might seem that this logic is irrelevant for Israel, in the sense that Israel does not have an extended deterrence problem. Alternatively, in some sense Israel might be seen as a recipient of extended deterrence from the United States, and the difficulty might therefore be seen to be relevant in that light. But I think the key point here is the "difficult" logic: the idea that you have to have large and varied forces, and to maintain a very high credibility that these will be used. This logic arises in Israel's case, not so much because of extended deterrence, but because of adjacency: the fact that Israel and its erstwhile foes live next door to one another. This was never really a problem for the Americans, because oceans always separated them from the Soviet Union. It has been much more a problem for others, say, for the relationship between the Chinese and the Soviet

Union, and for the Europeans. The problem of adjacency does create some difficulties similar to those of extended deterrence, in that it leads into the "difficult" logic through the need to guarantee that the nuclear threshold not become so high that other forms of warfare become possible under it. This could become very serious for Israel when it loses its regional nuclear monopoly.

The third situational factor I want to look at is the intensity of hostility. During the Cold War there was a generalized assumption that hostility was high, and this bears a very strong parallel with the circumstances in which Israel finds itself. If you have implacable foes and you have a real fear that war may break out, then deterrence logic is a justifiable and feasible approach.

The developments in East/West relations at the moment are moving away from this; therefore, wherever deterrence theory goes in relationship to its East/West thinking, it is probably going to be decreasingly relevant to the situation in which Israel finds itself, because tensions are lowering there, whereas clearly they are not here.

This problem of intense hostility points to a difficult paradox for deterrence theory, and this has to do with the idea of rationality. Deterrence is a bit like economic theory. It assumes rational actors. It assumes that people are behaving in some sort of sensible, calculated way, and that they have reasonably good information about the consequences of their choices.

But the problem in a situation of high hostility is that the assumption of rationality is weakened, because if hostility is extremely high, then irrational behavior, almost by definition, becomes more plausible.

Here one gets into a difficult circularity which has affected deterrence theory quite strongly, and which has led to the rather despairing remark of Herken that I quoted earlier, that, in a sense, deterrence theory can become a self-fulfilling prophecy. It can become a danger in its own right, particularly if deterrence theory becomes, as it were, a substitute for all other types of foreign policy.

Because deterrence theory requires massive threats to inflict genocidal destruction on opponents, it requires a fairly high degree of fear and hatred. It seems rather implausible to threaten somebody with complete obliteration unless you really hate them, or really fear them. In this sense the maintenance and plausibility of deterrence theory do require also the maintenance of high levels of hostility.

Therefore, within the evolution of deterrence theory there has been continuing concern that if deterrence logic, which is purely military logic, predominates in policy, it will lead to a self-perpetuating situation. The military policy that dictates that you have to meet a threat plays a considerable role in perpetuating the existence of that threat. It can rather easily foreclose any possibilities of political understandings and political agreements that might work to reduce the threat, and therefore reduce the need for deterrence.

One of the obvious ways in which this happens is that the logic of deterrence, as I have described it, and as it has evolved, has posed increasingly demanding technological requirements, and increasingly large military requirements. The pursuit of these large military requirements and the endless arms race that they generated, undercut the possibility, or at least made it much more difficult, for any kind of political understanding or political accommodation between the United States and the Soviet Union.

For a long time it was therefore a matter of concern that the pursuit of deterrence theory as policy, especially if deterrence theory was your **whole** policy, locked you into the current conflict situation and foreclosed possibilities for any kind of political accommodation.

And that, I think is an ongoing danger in deterrence policy.

I will make only one more small point, because it seems relevant to the current circumstances. There have been attempts to pursue the logic of deterrence away from non-war situations, and into situations where fighting was already occurring. This, of course, comes under the rubric of limited nuclear war, and the escalation problems that I described earlier. Now, inasmuch as there have been attempts to theorize here, what emerges very strongly is the extraordinary uncertainty of any kind of escalation control. The theory tells you almost nothing about this, because it is very unclear whether the conditions for rational calculation and, indeed, even sufficient information and command and control, can be maintained once one is in a nuclear war-fighting situation.

There is also the problem of loss of fear. Deterrence works as a war-prevention strategy because it creates fear in the mind of the opponent. But if fear has already been reduced because war is underway, then deterrence logic does not work.

This, I think was very clearly illustrated in the Second Gulf War that we have just witnessed. In the Iraqi Scud attacks on Israel, there was no kind of threat, or very little that Israel could offer as deterrence within this war-fighting situation, because the Iraqis were already being hit so hard that any additional pummeling was not going to make any difference. Therefore, under the circumstances, they had absolutely nothing or very little to lose in attacking Israel. This, I submit, is as good an illustration as any of the pitfalls in trying to apply the logic of deterrence within a war-fighting situation.

4. Between General and Immediate Deterrence

Bruce Russett

Basically, general deterrence is among the most important and still least systematically studied phenomena of international politics. Immediate deterrence is what happens when you get into a crisis--how do you deter the other side from attacking you in the crisis? General deterrence is preventing the crisis in the first place. General deterrence differs from immediate deterrence, because it focuses on the conditions under which a military diplomatic crisis may arise, rather than on the factors which determine the outcome of the crisis once it has erupted.

Why make this distinction? Is it just another example of academic hair-splitting? I think not. There are significant theoretical and methodological issues at stake. And all too often policy implications about deterrence are drawn--erroneously--from what is known about immediate deterrence, when what we may want to ask is what contributes to general deterrence. It is important to study general deterrence explicitly because the conditions affecting its success or failure may be very different from those affecting immediate deterrence.

The fact that the academic study of deterrence has focused primarily on immediate deterrence is ironic, because success in immediate deterrence is usually only a second-best solution for policymakers. That is, under most circumstances it would be better to prevent the crisis from emerging in the first place, than to pay the costs and take the risks of trying to deter one's adversary once the crisis has occurred. And yet, most systematic studies concern what happens in a crisis, rather than the prevention of a crisis from arising.

Let me now present some definitions, so that we are very clear about what we are discussing. A standard two-part definition of general deterrence is this: there is an adversarial relationship between two states in which leaders in at least one of those states would consider resorting to force to alter the status quo, and the other side, precisely because it believes the opponent would be willing to consider resorting to force, maintains forces of its own and offers warnings to respond in kind to attempts to use force contrary to its interests.

We are using the term "general deterrence" therefore, to characterize a situation in which the adversaries are neither using military force against one another, nor actively threatening to use it. Again, the situation depicted is before a crisis, an overt threat, has arisen.

In using the term "general deterrence" to characterize this situation, I do not wish to imply that the two adversaries are necessarily **deterred** from fighting, as that term is employed in rational deterrence models. That is, in this situation we are not necessarily implying that it is in fact the adversary's military capability and will to inflict substantial costs that prevent the attack. The attack may fail to happen because, for a variety of other reasons, the potential attacker--the challenger--does not have the positive incentive to attack. In other words, the real reason may or may not be primarily the negative incentive represented by its adversary's military capability.

The policy of general deterrence may succeed or fail in preventing a crisis, but we must not identify the mere absence of crisis as necessarily indicating successful deterrence. That a state may adopt a policy of general deterrence does not mean, in the absence of conflict, that the policy has succeeded simply because of the deterrer's military capability and will.

"Immediate deterrence" basically meets three conditions. Officials in at least one of the adversary states must actively be considering launching an attack on the other. Leaders of the other state must be aware of that and, to prevent such an attack, issue threats to retaliate. These threats and warnings most likely must be specific, communicated by official statements or by overt military actions ranging anywhere from broader troop reinforcements to large-scale mobilization.

A policy of general deterrence fails when the challenger couples a demand for change in the status quo with the threat of military force, or with the initiation of direct military action. Quite possibly the defender will respond with a counter-deterrent threat, in which case an immediate deterrence crisis occurs.

I will now give a five-stage account of a progression from peace to full-scale war. Doing so will make some of the distinctions clearer, and also make evident: (a) why it is important to draw these distinctions, and (b) why a failure to do so may give rise to some very erroneous policy recommendations.

1. We have a situation where a state adopts a policy of general deterrence by which it tries to deter another state from taking various steps to alter the status quo--steps that may require a commitment to extended deterrence by some ally or client state. Israel practices general deterrence all the time, and to some degree one could say that the United States practices general deterrence on behalf of Israel all the time. The former is probably more self-evident than the latter.

2. Another state, which I call the challenger, makes some military move or overt threat to change the status quo, a challenge that the general deterrent was intended to prevent. In other words, at this second stage the policy of general deterrence has failed, because the defender is now in a crisis that it was trying to prevent.

3. The defender now has to decide whether to strengthen a commitment to its own defense if its own territory is at stake, or to issue, reiterate, or enhance a commitment to an ally or a client. The defender will have to consider whether such a commitment would be worthwhile, including whether it would be provocative. At this point, the failure of the policy of general deterrence has produced a situation in which the defender must decide whether to adopt a policy of immediate deterrence.

4.   If the defender does so, then the challenger must decide whether to press ahead or retreat. If the challenger decides to press ahead, then we say that the policy of extended immediate deterrence has failed.

5.   If the policy of immediate deterrence has failed, the defender of the small ally has to decide whether or not to resist the attacker militarily. This may, indeed, be an open question, particularly in cases of extended deterrence where there is no threat to the defender's own territorial integrity, but rather only to that of its client or ally state. So the question in the final stage is: Does the big party defender in fact go to war when its policies of first general, and then immediate, deterrence have sequentially failed?

Why do we distinguish among all these stages? Because the difference between what works at one stage, and what works at another stage may be very great. For example, assume that we are at the stage of general deterrence and I, as defender, am trying to make credible to the challenger that I really mean to defend my ally. One way to try to make this threat credible, would be to establish a military alliance between myself (the defender) and the ally, which says to the challenger explicitly, overtly, publicly: If you challenge my ally, you will be in trouble.

This may be very effective most of the time. However, if it fails, and we move from general deterrence to crisis, and there is indeed an overt threat or challenge to this situation, we have come into a situation of immediate deterrence, and the deterrent effect of that alliance may now not be very great.

Why not? Because there is a very particular problem here, which is that general deterrence has failed despite the existence of the alliance. Therefore, the challenger has already discounted the effect of the alliance. The challenger has been sufficiently motivated to produce an immediate deterrence crisis, knowing that this alliance exists.

Under these circumstances then, if one looks empirically at the circumstances under which immediate deterrence succeeds and fails, one find a peculiar and anomalous result. The anomalous result is that immediate deterrence is more likely to fail when there is an alliance. And the reason is this selectivity of the first stage. General deterrence may perform very well in the presence of an alliance, but as we all know, **no kind of deterrence always works all the time**. Under circumstances where general deterrence has failed despite the existence of an alliance, that alliance has been discounted, and it no longer serves as a powerful deterrent in the immediate deterrent phase.

If, however, we push on to the last stage, the defender has to make the decision: Will I go to war now that not only general deterrence but also immediate deterrence has failed? Then the alliance comes in as a positive factor again, because here is a situation where, indeed, the defender has a public, overt commitment. Its prestige is on the line; its credibility in further crises is at stake; also, it probably has substantial moral commitments at stake, too. And so, under those circumstances, it is again likely that the defender will fight.

So you get this peculiar result, which is that the effect of alliance on deterrence situations varies depending on the particular point along the interaction process under review. The effect of an alliance or other kinds of signaling--and much of what goes on in deterrence is signaling through diplomacy or deployment of military forces--may be very different at different stages.

It is also important to recognize that in the analysis of deterrence we are often looking at circumstances where the exact reason or reasons why the attack or the crisis does not occur, if that is the case, may be obscure. **When deterrence fails, you know it; when deterrence succeeds, you may not know why it succeeded, and you may not even know that it succeeded**.

A standard example for this, at least in the America-centric deterrence literature, was Western Europe. Did general nuclear deterrence succeed in preventing a Soviet attack on Western Europe throughout the period from 1946 to 1988? I do not know. The Soviets did not attack. But that only means, necessarily, that deterrence did not fail. To assess whether deterrence succeeds requires asking: Did the Soviets ever intend to attack? If the answer is Yes, then deterrence succeeded. If the answer is No, then deterrence was irrelevant. And it is not obvious to me yet quite how one resolves that question.

Nor--even if we argue that deterrence did succeed and the Soviets probably did have an intention to attack--can one very readily say why deterrence succeeded. Did it succeed because of American nuclear capability? Did it succeed because of substantial western conventional capabilities, or for very different reasons?

That question about general deterrence is different from: Why wasn't there a war over Berlin, or why wasn't there a war over Cuba?

In a crisis, again, you know that general deterrence has already failed, and it is easier to say: Well, I'm now in a situation where I can ask whether immediate deterrence will succeed or fail, because at least there is an overt challenge. One can start with the assumption--it still has to be examined, but it is not an outrageous assumption--that the other side really does intend to try to attack here, and there is a real case that my response can prevent that attack. But in general deterrence it is less often obvious what the other side's intention was in the first place, and so it is not always clear whether general deterrence operates at all. The basic question: Has deterrence operated at all? poses a nasty analytical problem for immediate deterrence sometimes, and for general deterrence in particular.

How do you know when you are in a situation whether general deterrence is really operative? If you are an Israeli, do you think that general deterrence operated between Israel and Egypt up until the time of the Camp David Agreements? Almost surely you do, I expect. Since then, do you think general deterrence has operated between Egypt and Israel? Well, maybe yes, maybe no. As an outsider, I do not know what your answers would be to that. At least again it becomes problematic. Why it is important to split this hair is that we do not want to assume the problem away. One does not want simply to assume that the existence of superior military capability has prevented the war, if war may have been avoided for other reasons.

How do we handle this problem of making the fundamental analytical and ultimately policy error of assuming that it is always superior military force that actively deters? Professor Paul Huth and I, in grappling with this problem, decided that we would try to look at some situations where there was reasonable prima facie evidence to think that general deterrence really did operate.

We selected about a dozen enduring rivalries in the post-1945 world, cases of two states with longstanding disputes over competing claims to national territory, or where one party rejects the other's claim even to sovereignty. In these disputes one or both states actively seeks to alter the territorial status quo at various points in time. Not all enduring rivalries involve territory, but in the post-World War II period most of them have, and this is a good way to limit the scope of the investigation. We chose rivalries of at least 20 years in length, where over these 20 or more years there were at least five overt international disputes characterized by the threat or use of military force by central authorities. In other words, there were at least five years in which general deterrence did fail.

In effect, we have years in which deterrence has failed, but also significant years in which deterrence has not failed, simply because a major crisis has not erupted. So the question becomes: Over the range of years within each of these disputes, and also looking for similarities among the 12 dispute pairs, what characterizes those years in which general deterrence clearly failed, as distinct from those years in which general deterrence can be seen not to have failed.

Two of the rivalries are Arab-Israeli ones. The Israel-Egypt rivalry covers most of the period until about 1979, but then terminates because of the somewhat ambiguous situation after the 1978 Camp David Accords really took hold. Syria-Israel is considered a rivalry throughout the period. Other rivalries in different parts of the world include China and India; India and Pakistan; Argentina and Chile; some in Africa. A few of them involved nuclear weapons, but none of them were superpower rivalries, because there was no dispute between the United States and the Soviet Union over their own territories. Overall, we are looking at a spectrum of conditions going much beyond mere nuclear weapons.

Huth and I then looked at three kinds of explanations of why deterrence may fail. The usual explanation of deterrence success or failure essentially is the **rational deterrence model**. Beloved of American strategic theorists, the rational deterrence model argues that decisions to challenge the status quo by threat or use of military force can adequately be explained by reference to the military capability and will of the deterrer. What matters is that the deterrer have and exhibit the military capability and will to punish an attack.

A basic hypothesis of a rational deterrence model is that shifts in the military balance in favor of the defender will make challenges less likely, whereas shifts in the military balance in favor of the challenger will make challenge more likely. The core of the rational deterrence model is relative national power and especially military power. As the expected military costs of conflict increase to the challenger, the option of using military force is supposed to become less attractive.

So, how do we look at this empirically? One obvious way is to measure the **military balance**. Are years in which the military balance is less favorable to the defender years in which we are more likely to see general deterrence fail?

Variants of the rational deterrence model give us some other things to look at. Not just the static military balance, but power transitions or shifts in power. Does the challenger become emboldened by a military balance that begins to shift in his favor? Or, alternatively, does the challenger, seeing a military balance shifting against him, decide that it is now or never? Another variant of this is to ask whether there is an arms race going on. The argument says: The mere existence of an arms race, even if the relative balance between the powers does not change, with increasing military capability added every year, puts tensions and uncertainty into the rivalry, which may make it more likely for a crisis to occur. Yet another variant of a rational deterrence model would say: It also matters what is going on in other relationships. That is, if the challenger is faced with another dispute, not only with the initial one, it is unlikely to initiate a confrontation in the first dispute.

Alternatively, if the defender has another problem, is busy being distracted and paying attention to another rival, the first rival may be more likely to attack.

A second cut on this is to say, still within the purview of a rational model, that **domestic politics** also matter. That is, it is not just the international balance of power that matters, but a state may be more likely to challenge when it sees its rival in trouble domestically. Or maybe, more plausibly, a challenger may be more likely to make an overt military challenge under circumstances when the challenger government itself is having trouble at home, wanting some way to distract attention and divert hostility from domestic troubles to foreign troubles. So we look at the domestic political conditions within these states as well as what is going on internationally. In doing so, we hypothesize that a rational decisionmaker may rationally decide to issue a challenge in order to protect its domestic political base; it is still a rational decisionmaker.

The third model addresses the problem of **motivated misperceptions**, using psychological theories which depart from rational deterrence theory and say: Sometimes people make mistakes. They do not always perceive the military balance as accurately as they should to make rational decisions. And a particular variant is to say that they are more likely to make bad decisions when they are under other stressful political pressures. Suppose the challenger's military balance is unfavorable, and simultaneously he is threatened by widespread public discontent and even internal political upheaval because the domestic economy is in deep trouble.

Feeling desperate and looking for ways to get out of this problem, the challenger may misperceive the situation without even being fully or consciously aware of it, and believe that the military balance is less unfavorable than it is objectively. He is prone to view the military balance through more optimistic lenses because of great pressure at home to find a solution. The notion of motivated misperception cautions us that rational as well as accurate calculations of power are sometimes impossible when real-world government leaders are under terrible pressure, and therefore do not--indeed, cannot--make completely accurate assessments.

Having led the discussion this far, I briefly owe some answers. If we look at what amounts to about 300 years of challenge and response in interstate rivalries, what are the circumstances associated with failures of general deterrence?

First: power matters, and power matters a lot. This result in itself may not be surprising, but some of the details are more so. For example, the static balance of power matters some, but it is not a very powerful explanatory factor. Arms races also matter, and somewhat more strongly, in that one is somewhat more likely to see a failure of general deterrence after a period of intensive arms racing, rather than merely because the static military balance is unfavorable. Power transitions matter. When the power relationship has recently changed, a failure of deterrence is more likely.

Secondly, if the challenger sees the target, the defender, as undergoing domestic political difficulties, the challenger is **less likely** to challenge, not more likely. Arguably the challenger, being a smart, rational actor, anticipates that this is not a good time to put the other side under pressure, and fears that the defender might act irrationally--overreact.

Finally, there is also some evidence for motivated misperception. That is, under circumstances where domestic political troubles in the challenger state coincide with an unfavorable power balance, the challenger is more likely to mount an overt threat.

The advice for policymaking that follows from this analysis is: (a) Maintain, of course, the military power balance in your favor. (b) Worry about arms races, however, even if the power balance is in your favor. (c) Even if the power balance is in your favor, worry about power transitions and, ironically, not just a power gap that may be moving against you as defender, but even worry about a dynamic power balance that is moving in your favor, because the adversary may see the chances for his challenge slipping away. (d) Also look at what is going on elsewhere in the world. That is, if you as defender are indeed involved in a second dispute with another party, worry that you may well be more vulnerable to attack from your first challenger.

So there is a very complicated set of power relationships that matter here. The rational deterrence model explains a lot, but does not stop with counseling the obvious: namely, laboring to keep the power balance in your favor. There are many more subtleties, including all the dynamic changes that are happening.

Be alert for what is going on domestically within your challenger, and even within yourself, because these will affect how the adversary rationally calculates its chances.

And finally, worry about motivated misperception. Worry about something that is not easily controllable by you in military terms, because the irony is that two circumstances which might individually discourage an attack--a power balance in the defendant's favor, which by itself does discourage attack, and serious domestic political troubles in the challenger, which typically keep the challenger occupied, rather than lead to an overt challenge--may interact in ways that will encourage an attack. A defender can control the first of these, to some degree, by trying to maintain its military superiority; but the defender has little control over what is happening on the other side domestically.

Ironically, it is the conjunction of those circumstances, when the power balance is in your favor, but when the other government is in trouble domestically, which often leads to motivated misperceptions. This is when the rationality that one assumes for deterrence does not always hold, and the other side does not act as a rational decisionmaker ought to. Such become the unpropitious and sometimes uncontrollable circumstances where even the best-laid military analysis can still run into trouble, and result in the unraveling of elaborate, perhaps even elegant deterrence strategies.

5. Asymmetrical Deterrence

Athanassios G. Platias

This paper looks at the calculus of asymmetrical conventional deterrence from the standpoint of small states. For the purpose of this paper a small state is defined as one that has a narrow "power base" compared to the other state(s) with which it interacts, especially those with which it has conflicts, or others whose actions (or lack of them) have a direct influence on it.[1]

I argue here that in the confrontation of two unequal states, the small state's success in dissuading a possible attack is highly dependent on the strategy it adopts. The key to the success of an asymmetrical deterrence strategy is the potential opponent's sensitivity to cost. If the cost of his action is perceived to exceed a certain threshold, he is unlikely to attack. The challenge for the small state, therefore, is to appear willing and able to impose on its foes such an unacceptable cost.[2]

In line with this logic, this paper examines Greece's deterrence posture versus Turkey, especially its strategy for raising to an unacceptable level the diplomatic and military costs Turkey would pay for encroaching on Greek interests. Turkey constitutes the dominant regional power that is perceived to challenge the existing status quo.

Challenge from the Dominant Regional Power

Analysis of the threat. In response to perceived changes in its regional and domestic environments, since the early 1970s Turkey has adopted a revisionist foreign policy. Its policy seeks to alter the regional balance of power in its favor, and to ensure for itself a more important role as a regional power within the Western Alliance and in the Eastern Mediterranean.

At the level of Turkish-Greece relations, in the eyes of Greek political analysts this policy has assumed the dual form of a persistent challenge to the territorial status quo governing the Aegean (continental shelf, sea islands, and airspace), coupled with a continuous call for its renegotiation through bilateral agreements.[3] With the exception of the intractable Cyprus problem, these issues have dominated the agenda of Greek-Turkish relations over the past 18 years.

Subscribers to this revisionist thesis point to the current tension in Greek-Turkish relations, centering on the Muslim minority in Western Thrace, as an indication that human rights--an issue with great and ever-growing international appeal at the moment--have been added to the panoply of resources used by Turkey in promoting its broader revisionist policy in the region.[4]

This conceptualization of Greek-Turkish relations reflects two basic Greek premises: first, that Greece, since the end of World War II, has considered itself a status quo country; secondly, that a number of Turkish signals, statements, and actions since the early and mid-1970s at least lend themselves to an interpretation of being implicitly prejudicial to Greek security interests. These include: (a) statements by leading Turkish political figures concerning Greece or Greek-Turkish relations, that are considered threatening to Greek interests;[5] (b) Turkish diplomatic initiatives thought to undermine Greek sovereignty in the Aegean and Western Thrace;[6] and (c) Turkish military actions regarded as having negative security implications for Greece. Examples of such actions include the overall deployment of the Turkish armed forces, as well as the creation in 1975 of a new Turkish army corps (the Aegean Army), which is equipped with a large number of landing craft, is excluded from NATO command, and is positioned primarily along Turkey's Aegean littoral.[7]

Based on these threatening signals, and the recent historical experience--the 1974 Turkish invasion in Cyprus--Greek strategic analysts think that Turkey is likely to adopt a fait accompli diplomacy against Greece when the following two preconditions are fulfilled: (a) the opening of the "window of vulnerability" for Greece, that is, when Greece will not be capable or willing to resist Turkish encroachment, and (b) the opening of the "window of opportunity" for Turkey, that is, when it is unlikely that the powers will oppose a Turkish invasion.

Related to Greek concerns regarding Turkey's perceived role as a revisionist power in the region is the view, currently held in Athens, that Turkey has emerged as a beneficiary of recent international developments. Most frequently mentioned in this context are the Second Gulf War, the breakdown of Yugoslavia and the Soviet Union that has allowed Turkey to penetrate the Balkans and Central Asia, and the transfer of allied weapons from the central front to the flanks--all these have adversely affected Greek interests. Such developments have enhanced Turkey's role as the dominant regional power, and for as long as Greek-Turkish problems remain unresolved, have commensurately enhanced Greece's sense of vulnerability. In short, current Greek thinking includes an intensive and extensive view of the Turkish threat.

The perception of Turkish foreign policy aims and their implications for Greece cuts across party lines and forms part of a notable foreign policy consensus on the subject.[8] This is quite remarkable for a country in which partisan differences have long been reflected in sharply divergent party orientations in foreign policy matters.

Asymmetries. Threat, of course, is not perceived in a vacuum. Greek strategic thinking has been influenced by four important asymmetries: Greece's small population compared to that of Turkey, its geography, its comparatively meager economic resources, and superpower interest in the region. A brief review of each of these basic asymmetries follows.

Population. There are only ten million Greeks in Greece, with limited human military and economic resources. In contrast, Turkey's population is approximately 60 million. It is projected that by the turn of the century 11 million Greeks will have to face 73 million Turks.[9] Greece is, therefore, vastly outnumbered in terms of sheer manpower. Furthermore, Turkey has been able to maintain a huge standing army of more than 650,000 (excluding paramilitary forces[10])--an army potentially capable of making a swift transition to attack from its peacetime position. This army has a vast numerical superiority over its Greek counterpart. The manpower limitations make Greece vulnerable to surprise attack on the one hand, and to extended strategies for attrition[11] on the other.

Geography. Greece's geography hardly lends itself to defensive arrangements. The absence of strategic depth in the east (and the north) and the tremendous relative length of the border have plagued Greek strategists for a long time. Geography creates problems for Greece in all possible theaters of war with Turkey. Cyprus is 600 miles away from Greece, but only 60 miles from Turkey. Furthermore, major Greek islands are very close to the Turkish mainland. Important Greek population centers and military installations are within Turkish artillery range.

To complicate matters, the air defense of the Greek islands is extremely difficult because of the short warning time available for interception of penetrating enemy aircraft. Lastly, Greece's land border with Turkey in Thrace is far away from Greece's main strategic centers and access to it is limited due to the existing transportation network. In short, the geography of the Greek-Turkish land and sea borders do not give Greece the advantage of interior lines, that is, do not provide it with the capacity to rapidly concentrate forces on one front and then shift them to another.

Economic resources. Because of the sheer size of Turkey, Greece has always faced a disparity of economic resources. Until recently the Greeks believed that they might compensate for this disparity by generating a more advanced economy. This hope has diminished over the last decade due to Turkey's rapid economic growth and Greece's economic woes.

Great Power interests. External actors have a substantial impact on Greek-Turkish relations in various direct and indirect ways. The most important external actor is the US, which has had a strong interest in both sides. It seems, however, that Turkey is systematically considered more important than Greece in the American order of priorities.[12] This explains why the US tilts in favor of Turkey in almost every crisis. Hence, American interests in the area have conditioned Greek security concerns, and have defined the international constraints of the country.

Greek Strategy

The limits of external balancing. After the end of World War II, Greece--weakened by a decade of war, foreign occupation and civil conflict, and confronted with the bipolar logic of the Cold War--dealt with its security concerns solely within the Western Alliance.[13] The Turkish invasion of Cyprus in 1974 and the ensuing Greek-Turkish confrontation caused Athens to reconsider its traditional defense posture. At the root of this change in policy lay NATO's essential inaction during the Greek-Turkish crisis and the perception, deeply held among Greek civilian and military elites, that such inaction would leave the country dangerously exposed to a threat from the East, in case of a renewed conflict with Turkey.

In fact, the 1974 experience raised some broader questions. Like other small states, Greece had been obliged to trade off independence for security. In order to improve security and obtain protection, Greece had traded away some of its independence by joining NATO in 1952. But in 1974 Greek decisionmakers discovered that costs associated with the loss of independence through the alignment with NATO and the United States had not been commensurately offset by the benefits, namely, protection, that the Alliance was expected to provide. In short, the assessment of Greek policymakers was that the 1974 events had demonstrated that membership in the Alliance had not enabled Greece to move from insecurity to security. Rather, as events turned out, Greece had become both insecure and dependent.[14]

This realization led to a significant restructuring of Greek defense and foreign policy options. At the level of foreign policy, after 1974 Greece gradually sought to diminish its erstwhile one-sided dependence on the United States; it slowly turned to Europe for support for its foreign and security policies. The European orientation was consolidated with Greece's entry into the European Community in 1981. In the words of Constantine Caramanlis, whom many consider the chief architect of the 1974 Greek "shift toward Europe," membership in the European Economic Community (EEC) meant that "Greece, instead of remaining small and isolated, at the margins of international life, will become a part of the decisionmaking centers that have an impact on our fortune."[15]

The tilt toward Europe could not by itself solve the country's defense and security problems. But even in the absence of concrete security guarantees, the Greek presence in European institutions (e.g., EC, Western European Union [WEU]) has been viewed as an asset to the extent it increases the diplomatic costs and risks associated with an attack against the country. As Greek foreign policy analysts have noted, "the European Community was seen as a system of political solidarity capable of activating diplomatic and political levers of pressure to deter Ankara from potential adventures in the Aegean."[16]

The quest for internal balancing. The humiliation of the 1974 Cyprus crisis demonstrated to Greek policymakers that the defense posture designed by Greece's allies was not compatible with the country's interests, to say the least. The perceived Turkish threat consequently undermined the post-World War II Greek premise of relying on allies, and contributed to the Greek search for a more autonomous defense policy. Thus the underlying premise of post-1974 Greek defense policy became the principle that the country had to develop an autonomous security policy, drawing upon its indigenous resources to deal with the Turkish threat. In international relations theory this principle is commonly referred to as a strategy of internal balancing.[17] Hence, the country replaced external balancing (the expectation of allied reinforcements) with internal balancing (mobilization of the country's own resources).

The autonomous Greek defense policy within an allied context can be labeled a "NATO plus" strategy. It incorporates two types of arrangements. First, Greek armed units assigned to NATO are to regain their full independence from the alliance at any moment if Greece's vital interests are imperiled by Turkish actions. Secondly, forces under exclusive Greek national command are to be established. To implement the "plus" element of the "NATO plus" strategy, the post-1974 Greek governments took the following measures:

* Elite military units (i.e., the special forces) were strengthened and placed under exclusive Greek national command. In fact, the current ratio of special to regular forces in Greece is the highest among the NATO countries.

* Naval and air components (that had been neglected during the pre-1974 period) have been dramatically strengthened. This is clearly reflected in the budgetary allocations among the services where the Greek army's share of the budget has continuously declined, while the navy's and air force's share have increased.

* The Military High Command for Interior and Islands (ASDEN), which is not assigned to NATO, has been strengthened.

* The high degree of vulnerability resulting from dependence on foreign arms suppliers was minimized by adopting the counterdependency strategies of domestic production and diversification. Diversification proved to be a viable and quite effective strategy for reducing vulnerability dependence in a relatively short time. Within the last 15 years, the degree of dependence upon a single supplier has diminished from more than 80 percent in 1974 to approximately 40 percent in the 1980s.[18] Indigenous production, on the other hand, is a long term strategy. Currently, some 20 percent of the defense needs of Greece are satisfied by domestic production.[19] The long term objective is an equal division between imports and indigenous production.

Forms of asymmetrical deterrence. As a status quo country, Greece wants only to deter its opponents. Thus, the broad purpose of the Greek strategic posture is the deterrence of Turkish aggression.

Deterrence is a policy that seeks to persuade Turkey that the costs of using military force against Greece outweigh the benefits. Deterrence in Greece's strategic thinking takes four different forms:

national deterrence, international deterrence, extended deterrence, and active deterrence.

National deterrence. The Greek policy of deterrence seeks to present Turkey with a credible threat to exact a very high price in the event of aggression. This price can take many forms, including denial of battlefield objectives, and damage to military forces and other national assets through retaliation.

The credibility of the deterrent threat depends upon Greece being perceived as possessing (a) the military capability to inflict a burdensome cost on Turkey and (b) the will or the intention to use that capability as necessary.[20]

Deterrence is stronger when a state invests in cultivating its military might. In line with this principle, the post-1974 Greek governments have almost doubled domestic military expenditures. In particular, compared to any other NATO country Greece spends the highest percentage of its Gross Domestic Product--six to seven percent--for defense purposes. Another dimension of the resource allocation which must be taken into account is the share of manpower devoted to defense. Greece devotes more manpower to its defense-- approximately 6.1 percent of the labor force--than any other NATO country.[21]

The quest for quantitative symmetry with Turkey, however, has inherent limitations. As Greek Premier Andreas Papandreou mentioned in Parliament in January 1987, "our competition with Turkey along the quantitative dimension leads nowhere. Hence, emphasis should be given primarily to the qualitative improvement of our defense system in its entirety."[22] In fact, Greece seeks to achieve qualitative superiority over Turkey. Toward this end, the Greek government of the 1980s has taken measures which, inter alia, include: intensification of military training; emphasis on combined arms operations; use of capital-intensive systems of warfare; maintenance of a relatively modern arsenal; increased readiness and substainability; use of force multipliers such as Command, Control, Communication and Intelligence (C^3I) systems, and reduction of turnaround time for sorties.

In short, to counter its quantitative asymmetry, Greece's doctrine has placed emphasis on qualitative superiority. Coupled with intensive exploitation of the country's economic and manpower resources, this strategy has been expected to strengthen Greece's military capacity--the first requirement of deterrence.

The second requirement for a credible deterrence is the commitment to respond to an attack and, of course, the communication of that commitment. Indeed, successive Greek governments have repeatedly stated that "Greece claims nothing from any other country, but equally is not prepared to make any concession at the expense of its national territory."[23] To increase the clarity of its commitment, the Greek government has drawn some "red lines" in advance, namely casus belli. These serve as an automatic trigger of war or a large scale military action. The advance declaration of casus belli typically serves three general purposes: to lessen the possibility of miscalculation; to provide a clear signal that the deterrence has failed; and to establish a foundation of international legitimacy in the event of Greek military action (retaliation).

At least two casus belli have been explicitly stated by Greek governments: a Turkish attack on Cyprus, and any Turkish attempt to exploit the continental shelf on the Aegean.

International deterrence. Greece is a member of NATO and the EC, and it is in the process of becoming a member of the WEU. It also hosts several US and NATO bases on its territory. Participation in western institutions and western presence in the country have increased the costs and risks associated with an external attack against Greece.

One example will suffice to illustrate this point. Any attack on Greece from Turkey, and the resulting Greek-Turkish war, would inevitably result in the destruction of military installations and weapons (on both sides) that are partially or even exclusively financed by NATO and the United States for the purposes of common defense. Such a regional war would place the security of the US and NATO bases in Greece and Turkey at risk. Even a short (but intensive) war would completely wipe out NATO's infrastructure in the region. Hence, NATO and the US have every reason to try to deter any conflict between Greece and Turkey and, if deterrence fails, to intervene to stop it. This in turn, strengthens Greece's deterrence for as long as the country has adequate capacity to "rock the boat."

Extended deterrence. Greece's national interests extend beyond its borders to include the security of another state, namely Cyprus. As a result, when Cyprus is threatened by Turkish military action, decisionmakers in Athens must prepare to come to its defense by threatening retaliation against Turkey. This is the essence of the Greek strategy of extended deterrence. Yet to project the shadow of one's military forces into another country is a difficult task. As Thomas Schelling explains, "the difference between the national homeland and everything 'abroad' is the difference between threats that are inherently credible, even if unspoken, and threats that have to be made credible."[24]

The credibility of such an extended deterrence threat depends upon Greece's capacity to deny Turkish objectives in Cyprus, that is to employ adequate forces in a timely fashion in Cyprus. However, this is extremely difficult to achieve in this specific theater of war, since it is rather far away from Greece and much closer to Turkey. Hence, the credibility of Greece's extended deterrence in Cyprus is not based on the threat of denial but on a threat of retaliation, namely on the threat of all out war against Turkey. This is the meaning of the concept of "horizontal escalation" in current Greek strategic thinking. According to this concept, response to Turkish aggression need not be symmetrical (in the sense of reacting to the threat at the same location and level of the original provocation). "Horizontal escalation" implies an asymmetrical response which involves shifting the location or nature of one's reaction into a domain or terrain better suited to the application of one's strength against the adversary's weakness.

The credibility of the extended deterrent threat also depends on the will to fight, if necessary. Indeed, extended deterrence threats work better when the side making them has a track record of effectively defending its interests in similar situations in the past. In this regard, Greece's credibility suffers from its past behavior. Clearly Greece's performance was not up to par in 1974, hence the country damaged its reputation for defense. To reestablish the credibility of Greece's deterrence in Cyprus, Greek governments have adopted the following strategies:

* Casus belli: Greek governments have clearly drawn the "red line" on Cyprus. As Premier Andreas Papandreou declared in the Parliament in 1987: "in order to avoid misunderstanding, it should be known to friends and enemies alike that in case of an attack or invasion against the Greek-Cypriot positions, Greece will not stay out. I have warned that this is a casus belli. We hope that our partners in the EEC and our allies in NATO will understand the sincerity of our decision to defend Cyprus because if Cyprus is lost, Greece eventually will be lost."[25]

* Reputation for firmness and recklessness: In post-1974 crises Greece has proven that it can stand firm and, if necessary, take high risks (e.g., the March 1987 crisis). Indeed, extended deterrence threats work better when the side making them has built a reputation for being risk-seeking.

* Trip-wire: Greek forces have been stationed in Cyprus. Hence, any Turkish attack on that island would automatically involve the Greek forces positioned there. Naturally, this would drastically raise the likelihood of an all-out Greek-Turkish war.

Active deterrence. Active deterrence is the strategy of threatening or inflicting punishment on the opponent in order to dissuade him from continuing some undesired action. It threatens use of force to stop and possibly reverse an adversary from pursuing a course of action he has already undertaken. In essence this strategy involves initiating an action that can cease, or become harmless, only if the opponent responds by reversing his action. This strategy is illustrated by the actions taken by the Greek government in March 1987 in order to stop Turkey from exploring the Greek continental shelf in the Aegean.

55

In March 1987, Turkey's National Security Council ordered the oil exploration vessel Sismik to sail through the Dardanelles under naval escort to start oil prospecting in the Aegean. At the same time, the Turkish government published a map of the area the research vessel was supposed to explore, that made it immediately apparent that Sismik had been ordered to investigate the continental shelf in the Aegean claimed by Greece. Predictably, a crisis ensued. Greece considered such an infraction of its territorial rights as a casus belli. Thus, in response to the Turkish move, Greek armed forces were rushed to the eastern border (the Greek land border with Turkey) in a state of full alert.

To increase the credibility of its threat, the Greek government placed itself in a position from which it was difficult to retreat: it committed itself to a response by publicly putting on the line the nation's honor and diplomatic reputation.[26] Prime Minister Papandreou declared in an emergency television broadcast that "the maps published by Turkey show clearly that the planned route of the Sismik lies 95 percent within the area under which the Greek continental shelf extends.... It is our decision not to allow the Sismik to go on with its seismic research in the Aegean. It is our duty to defend both our borders and our sovereign rights." It was very fortunate, the Premier said, that this ship "has not showed up as yet in Aegean water." But if it did, and a war situation arose, he warned "a catalytic change might also occur in the entire Balkan area, even in the very defense system of the West, that is NATO itself."[27]

Clearly, the Greek government had decided to run the risk of unilateral escalation by declaring general mobilization and issuing orders to the navy to sink the Turkish vessel. These could have precipitated an equally forceful response by Turkey. As a result, the pace of military events could have outstripped the time needed for diplomacy to come into the picture. But it is precisely the manipulation of the risk of war that made deterrence work. The initiation of the process that carried the risk of disaster for both sides contributed to Turkey's decision to take a step backward.

The March 1987 crisis demonstrated that striking a balance between deterrence stability and credibility is a demanding task. A stable deterrence posture must maintain a delicate balance of demonstrating resolve and readiness to use force without at the same time provoking the opponent.[28] Establishing the credibility of deterrence is also a difficult task. For credibility enhancement it is usually crucial to demonstrate firmness. This implies the need to issue threats and adopt an uncompromising bargaining position. Yet there are serious risks associated with this course of action (e.g., provocation, escalation). No wonder, therefore, that in practice, achieving an effective balance between credibility and stability has proved to be a precarious task for policymakers.[29]

Greek strategists try to design a deterrent posture that is both stable and credible. Three basic options are available to Greece: **intransigent strategy**, that is, adoption of a firm and unyielding position vis-a-vis Turkey; **firm-but-flexible strategy**, that is, adoption of a mixed strategy of standing firm in response to the Turkish demands while offering compromise based on reciprocal accommodation; and **appeasement strategy**, that is, adoption of a strategy of unilateral concessions vis-a-vis Turkey.

The problem inherent in an intransigent strategy is that Greece's deterrence credibility is maximized at the expense of deterrence stability. This means that the chances of escalation are high. In addition, an intransigent stance by Greece may discredit the moderate policymakers in Turkey who advocate compromise and, instead, enhance the position of Turkish hard-liners (e.g. the military establishment). An appeasement strategy, on the other hand, avoids the problems associated with an intransigent stance, and thus strengthens deterrence stability. However, unilateral concession may encourage further Turkish demands. Thus, appeasement is an effective strategy only if the adversary is motivated solely by defensive goals. Turkey is clearly not motivated by defensive goals. It aspires to change the prevailing status quo in the region. Consequently, Greek policymakers have concluded that the policy of appeasement--sacrificing a great deal to avoid war--is dangerous.[30] The credibility of Greece's commitment would be weakened and thus Turkey might be tempted to attempt further coercion.

For Greece the most effective stance is therefore believed to be a mixed strategy in which opposition to the demands of Turkey is coupled with conditional compromise.[31] This firm-but-flexible strategy was adopted in the March 1987 crisis. At that time, Greece demonstrated its determination to escalate via mobilization and preparation of a preemptive strike, and subsequently accepted a compromise to break the deadlock: it gave assurances to Turkey that Greece, too, would refrain from drilling in disputed areas. The Greek conditional offer of compromise signaled to the Turkish leadership the possibility of taking the necessary step backward without damaging its bargaining reputation and its domestic position. Had Greece not taken this position, and had it not offered a face-saving way out, the Turkish leadership might have found it difficult to retreat under pressure.

Conclusion

To seek allies is a time-honored way to compensate for a state's small size. **External balancing**, namely the added strength in "borrowing" the power of the other states, may be used for deterrence, and for defense if deterrence fails. Protection is, therefore, the primary motivation for seeking allies. However, the small state has every reason to wonder whether, if the need arises, the great power ally will honor the commitment to defend its smaller partner. Past experience suggests that this is an uncertain prospect. The Greek experience in particular suggests that the Atlantic Alliance was either unwilling or unable to provide Greece protection against the threat from Turkey.

Yet participation in international institutions such as NATO and WEU may be an asset to a small state such as Greece even in the absence of secure guarantees. This holds true to the extent that such participation increases the diplomatic costs and risks associated with an attack against the country. Hence, it indirectly strengthens deterrence.

The safest way to increase the cost of aggression to an opponent is by **internal balancing**, through mobilization of the country's own resources. This however implies heavy emphasis on military spending, allocation of significant manpower to defense, and so on. Naturally, emphasis needs to be placed upon deployment of cost effective methods to limit the burden.

The utility of military manpower can be maximized by choosing weapons technology that tends to maximize the efficiency of fighting men. **Qualitative superiority** is one way to get the most out of a small population. To maximize deterrence without having to match in quantity the forces of the adversary requires deployment of superior technology, military organization, tactics, operational methods and strategy.

In the final analysis, the anarchical nature of the international system creates a serious security problem for all states, and those with limited capabilities operate within narrow margins. Yet, even in asymmetrical confrontations small states may succeed in dissuading possible aggression provided they adopt certain strategies. How small states bargain, adopt and implement their national security strategies can make a difference between success and failure, between winning and losing. Choosing a clever mix of strategies--one that is best tailored to unique conditions and circumstances--is the key to success.

Notes

1. For an extensive discussion on the definition of the term "small state" see Athanassios G. Platias, "High Politics in Small Countries: An Inquiry into the Security Policies of Greece, Israel and Sweden." PhD Dissertation (Cornell University, 1986), Appendix.
2. See Olav Knudsen, "Asymmetric Deterrence: Norway versus the Soviet Union." Paper presented at a Conference on "Small States Strategies: Managing Threats and Dependence" (Delphi, May 10-12 1991), p. 7. Also, D. Mark Kilgour and Frank C. Zagare, "Asymmetric Deterrence." Paper presented at the International Studies Association (Washington DC, April 10-14, 1990).
3. Van Coufoudakis, "Greek-Turkish Relations, 1973-1983: The View from Athens," *International Security*, vol. 9, no. 4 (Spring 1984), pp. 201-204.
4. See *Ôá ÍÅÁ* (Daily), February 14, 1990, p. 11.
5. For pertinent examples see *Greece: A Profile* (Athens: International Studies Association, 1988), Appendix I, p. 33; and *Turkish Officials Speak on Turkey's Aims* (Athens: Institute for Political Studies, 1985).
6. For an analysis of this point see Andrew Wilson, *The Aegean Dispute*. Adelphi Paper 155 (London: International Institute of Strategic Studies, 1975).
7. See *Journal of Parliamentary Debates* (*Praktika Voulis*) (Greek), May 24, 1987, p. 6420; and Robert McDonald, "Alliance Problems in Eastern Mediterranean--Greece, Turkey and Cyprus: Part II," in *Prospects for Security in the Mediterranean*. Adelphi Paper 229 (London: International Institute of Strategic Studies, 1988), p. 74.
8. For the most recent view on this see Van Coufoudakis, "Greek Political Party Attitudes toward Turkey: 1974-1989," in D. Constas, ed., *Greek-Turkish Conflict toward the 1990s* (London: Macmillan, 1991).
9. For a projection of the Turkish population see *Turkey: A Country Study* (Washington DC: Library of Congress, 1988), p. 378.
10. See *The Military Balance, 1989-1990* (London: International Institute of Strategic Studies, 1989), p. 76.

11. Because of its great superiority in human resources, Turkey could benefit from any military encounter that reduced Greek military strength even if its own losses were much higher, so long as the ratio of Turkish to Greek losses does not exceed the overall ratio of strength in its favor.

12. See for example, Jed Snyder, *Defending the Fringe: NATO, the Mediterranean and the Persian Gulf* (Boulder, CO: Westview Press, 1987).

13. Yannis Roubatis, "The US Involvement in the Army and Politics in Greece, 1946-1967." PhD Dissertation (Johns Hopkins University, 1980).

14. See Platias, *High Politics in Small Countries*, pp. 146-175.

15. *Kathimerini* (Daily), January 1, 1981.

16. Yiannis Valinnakis, *The Security of Europe and Greece* (Greek) (Athens: Foundation of Political Studies and Training, 1988), p. 55.

17. See Kenneth Waltz, *Theory of International Politics* (Reading, MA: Addison-Wesley, 1979), p. 168.

18. See the yearly reports of the US Arms Control and Disarmament Agency, *World Military Expenditures and Arms Transfers*.

19. Data presented to the parliament by the Greek Prime Minister. See *Journal of Parliamentary Debates* (Greek) (January 23, 1987), p. 2915.

20. For the classic formulation of the requirements of deterrence, see William Kaufmann, *The Requirements of Deterrence* (Princeton, NJ: Center for International Studies, 1954), pp. 6-8.

21. See *NATO Press Service,* Press Release, M-DPC-2 (86) 39 (December 4, 1986).

22. See *Journal of Parliamentary Debates* (Greek), January 23, 1987, p. 2914.

23. See the announcement of the new defence policy, ÔÁ ÍÂÁ (Greek) (January 9, 1985), p. 18.

24. Thomas Schelling, *Arms and Influence* (New Haven, CT: Yale University Press, 1986), p. 36.

25. See *Journal of Parliamentary Debates* (Greek), January 23, 1987, p. 2914.

26.	For a theoretical analysis of this tactic see Edward Rhodes, *Power and Madness* (New York: Columbia University Press, 1989), pp. 107-34.
27.	*ÔÁ ÍÅÁ* (March 28, 1987), pp. 14-15.
28.	For an analysis of this problem see Richard Smoke, *War: Controlling Escalation* (Cambridge, MA: Harvard University Press, 1977), pp. 239-97; and Robert Jervis, *Perception and Misperception in International Politics* (Princeton: Princeton University Press, 1976), pp. 58-113.
29.	For an analysis of this problem see Paul Huth, *Extended Deterrence and the Prevention of War* (New Haven, CT: Yale University Press, 1988), pp. 11-14 and 33-55.
30.	In fact in the Greek strategic debate the term "appeasement" is used with the pejorative connotations that derive from the Munich debate. See *Journal of Parliamentary Debates* (Greek), May 24, 1987, p. 6240.
31.	For a theoretical analysis of the advantages of this strategy, see Glenn Snyder and Paul Diesing, *Conflict Among Nations: Bargaining, Decision Making and System Structure in International Crises* (Princeton, NJ: Princeton University Press 1977), pp. 254-80; Huth, *Extended Deterrence*, pp. 51-5; and A. George, D. Hall and W. Simons, *The Limits of Coercive Diplomacy* (Boston, MA: Little, Brown, 1971).

6. The Limits of Deterrence Theory

George W. Downs

One of the chief difficulties in evaluating the state of deterrence theory is the absence of consensus about just what "it" is. In its most popular incarnation it is nothing more than the assertion that a state will refrain from an act when the expected benefits are less than the expected costs or, more precisely, when the expected discounted net benefits are less than those associated with the status quo. If benefits and costs are interpreted broadly enough, this is both eminently reasonable and virtually nonfalsifiable. Any prediction error can simply be credited to an omitted cost or benefit. This version of deterrence theory is also of limited use to policymakers who need to know--at the very least--something about which benefits and costs need to be manipulated and how much. In the absence of this information, we have the equivalent of a marketing theory that says that consumers will balance quality, cost and the availability of substitute goods when making a purchase. True, but not particularly helpful.

Deterrence theorists are aware of this weakness, and spend a great deal of time thinking about more precise specifications and the impact of complicating factors. The latter include not only particular benefits and costs, but a host of other things such as beliefs and intentions, misperception, discount rates, command and control problems, the past history of interaction between the parties, and the political organization of the states.

Scholars who say something about how any of these affect a state's response to deterrence attempts on the part of another state make a contribution to deterrence theory, and they have been extremely active in recent years. We now know far more than we did just a decade ago about the role of utility and information uncertainty, the role of capability estimates, reputation, crisis bargaining, and escalation. As is true in economics, the inspiration for much of deterrence theory, it has been easier to talk about the direction of an effect than its magnitude, but the progress is still undeniable.

The limits of this progress are also undeniable, however, particularly in the sense of providing a basis upon which policymakers can confidently base strategic decisions. Theoretical insights are rarely integrated into a single model and tend to be very abstract. Empirical studies conducted to test and refine theoretical propositions are plagued by measurement problems and selection effects. In what follows we will examine the difficulties these limitations pose in connection with two specific questions: the use of deterrence in crises, and the security (or insecurity) that results from mutual arms buildups.

Summarizing Deterrence Success

Since the goal of this chapter is to provide a general picture of the limits of deterrence, it might appear to be useful to begin by summarizing the historical experience of those states that have employed the strategy. This should tell us something about when deterrence will be successful and the reasons why it fails. Understanding why this approach is not advisable provides a useful introduction to the limitations of empirical tests of deterrence theory.

One problem is that scholars find it difficult to agree on the universe of deterrence successes because they disagree on what would have happened in its absence (i.e., the counterfactual). Did the United States successfully deter the Peoples' Republic from invading Taiwan during the 1950s? Huth and Russett argue that the answer is yes.[1] They believe that the probability of the People's Republic attacking the island would have been far higher without an active deterrent policy on the part of the US. Lebow and Stein take the counter-position. They contend that there is little or no direct evidence that the People's Republic ever intended to invade and that, in fact, it viewed its own buildup along the coast as a deterrent to US invasion during the Truman administration.[2] Since Lebow and Stein believe there would have been no war in the absence of the US presence (their estimation of the counterfactual), they view it as neither a success nor failure of deterrence--the equivalent of giving the anti-cancer drug to a healthy patient.

And this is only the beginning. Those opposed to deterrence want positive evidence that aggression has been contemplated, because they do not want mutual indifference coded as a deterrence success. Yet a proponent of deterrence could argue that insisting that there be evidence that a state has actively considered the use of force before deterrence can be viewed as having taken place creates a significant bias. Not only does it ignore the fact that the potential attacker has a strong incentive to deceive its victim about the attacker's true intentions,[3] but this requirement ignores the role of expectations. Ideally, a state would like deterrence to be so successful, that the expectation of failure or excessive cost keeps military intervention from being seriously considered. If we require that serious planning take place, we will be examining only the instances where there has already been partial deterrent failure. Many instances of deterrence success will never be considered, and the effectiveness of the strategy will be seriously underestimated.

On the surface it might seem that the task of identifying deterrence failures would be far easier, but this too presents problems. One is deciding whether deterrence has really been attempted. Did Argentina's invasion of the Falklands represent a deterrence failure, or was Britain simply not paying very much attention? How about Iraq's invasion of Kuwait? What about situations where deterrence may have been partially but not totally successful? Israel did not deter the use of Scud missiles against it during the Gulf War, but did it deter the use of troops and other weapons? Scholars try to avoid such problems by setting a threshold (e.g., number of troops killed) for success and failure, but this device has little theoretical justification. It is one thing to call central bank monetary policies designed to prevent economic downturns less than completely successful, and quite another to call them completely unsuccessful. Just as a brief recession is not a depression, a small conventional war is not a total war. If deterrence can reliably reduce the magnitude of conflict, it is important to know this.

An even deeper issue lies in deciding whether deterrence policy has failed or whether it has been ineptly or poorly implemented. Critics of deterrence tend to view this distinction as unimportant or, worse, simply a ruse by which deterrence advocates can avoid failure. If deterrence does not work, what better protection against falsification than to claim that the threat was too small or was badly communicated? This sort of defense can bear a striking similarity to the claims of the rainmaker that his magic failed only because the people of the town did not have enough faith.

The frustration is understandable, but the implementation of defense should not be dismissed out of hand. While we tend to talk about deterrence as if it were a rigorously defined set of procedures that is equivalent to taking 600 milligrams of a given drug once a day for three weeks, it is not. It is a broad term that incorporates anything designed to raise a prospective opponent's cost of aggression. Always claiming that deterrence would have worked if implemented correctly may be exasperating, but to insist that a state that has increased its coastal defenses is doing the same thing as a state that arms itself with nuclear weapons is hardly an improvement.

The basic problem is that "deterrence strategy" is no more homogeneous a category than macroeconomic intervention, chemotherapy, or a diet program. While there will inevitably be an average effectiveness for all of these prescriptions, those making the decision to employ them have the ability to make finer distinctions and have little use for aggregate performance statistics that ignore what they believe are salient aspects of their particular context. Very few members of the Federal Reserve Board would be interested in the work of an economic analyst who cautioned against a cut in interest rates to stimulate the US economy because cuts in the money supply had failed to control inflation in Latin America. Very few defense department officials are interested in comparable claims about deterrence success.

The best way around this problem is to work with specific categories of deterrence that are meaningful to policymakers and seem homogeneous enough to yield useful generalizations. Immediate deterrence and arms races are two such categories.

Deterrence in Crises

The weakness of deterrence about which there is the most widespread agreement is its tendency to provoke as well as to restrain in time of crisis. The events that led to World War I remain the most frequently cited example of how this can work. Germany's aggressiveness was, in large part, an exaggerated response to the deterrent efforts of France and Russia.[4] Critics of deterrence argue that a host of other examples fall into the same broad category. For example, Lebow and Stein argue that the American strategy of freezing Japanese assets and imposing an oil embargo "created a mood of desperation in Tokyo, an essential precondition of the attack on Pearl Harbor that followed."[5] The same authors see the Cuban missile crisis as having been precipitated by a combination of Soviet strategic inferiority and Kennedy's bellicose attempts at deterrence. A similar security dilemma-driven process is assigned responsibility for the 1967 War: Egypt mobilized to deter an attack on Syria which led to Israeli mobilization and what some interpret as a preemptive first-strike by Israel.[6]

Defenders of deterrence see the same potential problem, but believe it occurs more rarely than critics of deterrence contend. They also insist that it can be overcome by the intelligent application of a balanced approach to deterrence based on the principle of reciprocity or Tit For Tat. For example, while acknowledging the existence of the security dilemma, Huth argues that it is most likely to occur if the defender overreacts and initiates rapid escalation during the early stages of a crisis. This rapid response produces an equally rapid reaction from the other side, and the pace of events quickly outstrips the time necessary for careful diplomacy. This, he believes, is what occurred both in Europe in 1914 and in the Middle East in 1967.[7]

Huth backs up his claim with both case material and aggregate data analysis. Using a sample of 58 cases of extended, immediate deterrence, he finds that the "adoption of a tit for tat policy by the defender increased by 33 percent the probability of successful deterrence as compared with failing to match or exceeding the military escalation of the potential attacker."[8]

These are impressive results, but caution is necessary in gauging the effectiveness of a strategy through aggregate statistics. As is always the case, there is the possibility of a selection effect. That is, there could be systematic differences between the cases in which Tit For Tat was used, and the cases where it was not. It does not seem outside the realm of possibility that a state that was both sufficiently strong and convinced it was fighting a very hostile opponent would adopt an aggressive deterrent strategy and that the strategy would fail because **any** strategy would fail. Similarly, a weaker state might choose appeasement out of an inability rather than a desire to choose another course.

How much emphasis an analyst places on the possibility that deterrence efforts may provoke instead of restrain is always closely tied to the estimated likelihood of misperception and misinterpretation. Backed up by a wealth of experimental evidence, those with a psychological orientation have no difficulty producing examples of motivated behavior and attribution biases.

> Our analysis of case studies of adversarial relationships indicates that the expectations that deterrence has about deterrer and challenger bear little relation to reality. Challengers frequently focus on their own needs and do not consider, or distort if they do, the needs, interests, and capabilities of their adversaries.... Deterrers, in turn, may interpret the motives and objectives of a challenger in a manner consistent with their expectations, with little regard to the competing expectations of the challenger. Both sides may also prove insensitive to each other's signals.[9]

Many of these claims are persuasive. We have only to pick up a newspaper to see examples of a state interpreting its own behavior in the most generous light, while insisting that anything a rival does is intentionally aggressive and provocative. What is less clear is whether the cumulative effect of such distortions renders deterrence completely ineffective or simply reduces its effect somewhat. Since no competing model based on psychological biases and heuristics has been constructed and tested with data, it is difficult to test the strength of these claims.

Those concerned about the provocative impact of deterrence policy, counsel replacing it with something supplying more positive incentives. The most well-known of these is the aforementioned Tit For Tat. But this strategy has its detractors. It is vulnerable to uncertainty and can result in an endless echo of punishments and retaliations that had their original source in a misperception. Another problem lies in interpretation: a state may see another state's gesture as being more aggressive than its own, and escalate accordingly. It is probably to prevent such confusion that confidence-building gestures in the 19th and 20th centuries have usually involved a small number of specific weapons systems. This was true of the Anglo-German and Anglo-French naval races and, until very recently, true of the arms race between the US and the Soviet Union.

Critics such as Lebow and Stein favor other methods of what they call reassurance. For Tit For Tat they would substitute Graduated and Reciprocated Initiatives in Tension Reduction (GRIT).[10] This technique encourages more unilateral gestures of cooperation than Tit For Tat, and is hence less conservative. They also favor reassurance through a gesture of "irrevocable commitment" which provides unambiguous evidence of good will.

The archetypical example of this gesture is Sadat's trip to Israel.

While undeniably useful in certain contexts, these and similar methods have an important limitation. In recognizing that a small or isolated gesture will rarely convince a state that its rival is sincere, they are sensitive to the needs of the state on the receiving end of the signal. They are less sensitive to the needs of the state sending the signal. The problem lies in the expected cost and benefit of the action. Simulation suggests that a state will rarely make a dramatic gesture of cooperation when there is a substantial chance that its rival will ignore it, and this is often the case.[11]

This helps explain why techniques like GRIT and dramatic, irrevocable gestures have been so little used in the past. It also suggests that the complex equilibrium calculations that are often required in rational deterrence theory are worth undertaking because they can uncover motives that are initially unclear. In this case, it suggests that states are not withholding gestures of cooperation simply because of biases induced by a lengthy confrontation or arms race, but because it is rational to do so. If this is true, the probability that they will respond to recommendations to change their behavior seems slight.

Grand gestures will occur only when the cost of making them is not so great as it might first appear, or when the likelihood that they will be reciprocated is very high. Arguably, both conditions were met when Gorbachev announced the troop reduction and force restructuring that took place in Eastern Europe in 1989. He had less inclination to seek offensive advantage on the European front, and good reason to believe that public opinion in West Germany and other countries had shifted in such a way that it would be impossible for NATO not to respond to a Soviet troop reduction with a reduction of its own. Such conditions are likely to be rare.

This does not mean that the idea of positive signals should be abandoned; only that there may be a good reason to believe they will often be modest. This realization has the virtue of tempering expectations and avoiding the inference that the absence of a grand gesture means unwillingness to cooperate. It also sensitizes us to the need to better understand positive strategies and the ways that positive strategies interact with negative ones.

In sum, the potentially provocative character of deterrence is universally acknowledged, and modern deterrence theory proscribes against heavy-handed attempts to achieve greater and greater superiority. Instead, it advocates reciprocity (or something more generous depending on the circumstances) and a variety of crisis stabilizing and "firm but fair" bargaining techniques that evidence flexibility but not weakness. An opponent of deterrence theory can claim that this enlightened version of deterrence is not really deterrence at all since it succeeds by positive inducement as well as the fear of punishment. This point is narrowly true, but mostly beside the point. Ultimately, policy prescription is what matters.

Yet questions remain in areas of central interest to the policymaker. Can the success rate of about 85 percent discovered by Huth be trusted to imply that this rate holds in all situations? Should the decisionmaker pay no attention to the variables not included in Huth's model? Can this enlightened version of deterrence be improved upon by more positive reinforcement? Is the meaning of Tit For Tat and Firm but Flexible bargaining always clear? These and other questions like them create the limits of deterrence theory in crisis decisionmaking.

Arms Races and Deterrence

Scholars have long differed on the issue of whether arms races provoke or deter conflict. Where traditional deterrence theory emphasizes the effect of arms race behavior on demonstrating capabilities, resolve, and the cost of aggression, the security dilemma perspective emphasizes its effect on goal perceptions and, implicitly, expectations about the ability of national resources to absorb the cost of continued peace.

The difference in emphasis leads to different predictions about the consequences of arms races and how they should be conducted. A relatively equal arms race is nonthreatening from a deterrence standpoint, because it demonstrates mutual resolve and increases the cost of initiating conflict for both parties. Deterrence theory recognizes the temptation to engage in preventive war that will occur if one side begins to run out of resources, but it holds out the possibility that the arms buildup will have made the cost of conflict so great that the impact of superior resources will be attenuated. This is why theorists sometimes speak in terms of a threshold of maximum acceptable cost, and it is the basis for the common belief that MAD (mutual assured destruction) creates a situation that is extremely stable. From a security dilemma standpoint, things look very different. Even an equal arms race is dangerous because it convinces each side of the other's aggressive intent. As the pace of the race continues to escalate in a vain attempt to increase security, war is viewed as increasingly inevitable. The side with fewer resources faces a choice of fighting sooner at equal odds, fighting later at a great disadvantage, or capitulating.

Empirical research on the topic is inconclusive. Among the more recent studies, Diehl[12] found that the conditional probability of a dispute preceded by an arms race turning to war appeared to be somewhat greater than one that was not preceded by an arms race, but the difference was quite small. When Diehl and Kingston[13] examined the more basic question of whether a military buildup increases the chances that a militarized dispute would occur in the first place, they found no evidence to support a relationship.

Findings that suggest that arms races and war may be unrelated are provocative because we expect that states that anticipate conflict will be much more likely to engage in an arms race than those which do not. Such in all likelihood will comprise the better part of any arms race data set, thereby creating a bias that gives the impression that arms races lead to war whether they really do or not. The absence of a relationship argues that arms races are deterring war rather than increasing its likelihood.

Once again, however, we need to be cautious about concluding too much from aggregate data. Case studies make it clear that the decision to build arms is a strategic move inextricably bound to each state's goals, resources, satisfaction with the status quo, and expectations about the future. Those who engage in aggregate data analysis are attempting to evaluate the strategy of arms racing, but what they are actually assessing is the outcome of a mixture of strategies, games (internal as well as external), and perceptions. While it is interesting from a historical point of view to know whether arms races have generally led to war or not, the implication that the answer to this question has strategic value depends on whether there is any reason (a) to believe that the past mixture of strategies, games and perceptions is likely to characterize the future; and (b) to assume that a real-life strategic situation is likely to take place in an environment where the players have no **useful** information about the utilities and perceptions beyond that which can be inferred from historical patterns.

Both propositions are almost certainly wrong. While the future blend of strategies, games, and perceptions may be the same as in the past, there is good reason to believe that it will not be. The arms race contexts that characterized the first half of the 20th century could not have been extrapolated from the last half of the 19th century, much less the previous 200 years. Even if we make the heroic assumption that the distribution of preferences for expansion, resources, and misperception is the same, the technology of war has changed in such a way that the costs associated with Great Power wars have risen dramatically. Regardless of one's skepticism about expected utility models, it is difficult to envision a world where cost has **no** implication for the likelihood that arms races will lead to war or successful deterrence. Analysis based on data from the entire set of arms races that have taken place since 1850 (or 1900) does not take this into consideration. It is as if someone proposed to make a general statement about the relative impact of a college education on expected lifetime earnings and sought an average figure for the period 1900-1991. The average figure may be of use to a social historian--especially when comparing various nations--but the changes in the economy of any single country and the percentage of people with a college education would mean that the "average" figure would have little enduring stability or policy significance. The likelihood that arms races will lead to war will keep changing for a variety of similar reasons, and the average likelihood is no more meaningful.

The more critical point again concerns the relationship between strategy and context. Relying on aggregate historical information to infer the wisdom (or folly) of any deterrence strategy makes sense only if we can attain a predictive accuracy that satisfies the needs of the decisionmaker or is based on a demonstrated incapacity to do better using more detailed information. In the case of arms races, neither requirement is satisfied. We do not yet have an empirical model which accurately predicts which arms races lead to war, and we have not yet begun to demonstrate the irrelevance of factors such as whether the arms race is nuclear or nonnuclear and whether a rival leader's objectives seem more reminiscent of Woodrow Wilson or Hitler.

One way of coping with this dilemma is to return to the historical record and attempt to construct a data set that includes the variables that policymakers and theorists believe are relevant. This, however, poses countless problems. Even the most gifted team of contemporary historians would have a difficult time estimating US and Soviet priorities during the past 40 years, the perception each had of the other's priorities, the arms strategy each was employing and how it was perceived, and so forth. To compile similar data about the arms race between Argentina and Chile (1890-1902) or between Great Britain and France (1840-1866) would be an even more formidable task.

Another approach is to use rational deterrence theory and simulation to explore the consequences of different arms strategies under different assumptions. This has proved to be helpful in a piecemeal fashion, but there are few models that possess the three minimal attributes that we require of a formal theory that deals with the relationship of arms races to war. These attributes are: (a) the existence of two reacting, strategy-generating opponents; (b) specification of the conditions under which deterrence is sustainable; and (c) the explicit incorporation of arms increases (and decreases) as a decision variable that is tied to the probability of war.

Arms race models in the Richardsonian tradition are a good example of formal models that have little to do with deterrence and possess none of the necessary attributes. Here the rate of growth of one nation's arms stock is a linear function of the arms stocks of the two participating sides. For certain values of the parameters, this system of equations is stable, meaning that any trajectory tends toward a point where the rates of change are both zero. For other values, trajectories diverge and arms stocks increase without bound at an increasing rate.[14] Implicitly, Richardson and those who have followed his approach have identified the second situation as leading inevitably to war.

Although it is possible to reexpress a Richardson-like arms race as a differential game,[15] it is basically a deterministic process that involves no strategic choices on the part of either participant. The outcome is strictly a function of initial conditions. While Richardson hoped that nations would come to their senses and act in such a way as to overcome the model's implications, the decisions that they would need to make are not included in the model. This specification means that the Richardson model has little to offer from the standpoint of prescription. No mitigating strategies are possible. It also embodies an a priori assumption that an arms race has no independent impact on the probability that war will occur. War may or may not occur, but whether it does or not is wholly a function of the initial conditions. The model leaves no room for a counter-factual.

Richardson's model also lacks an explicit theory of deterrence. He simply assumes war will eventually occur whenever a trajectory fails to converge to a point where the rate of change is zero. War is not so much predicted as anticipated to be the most likely outcome when the enormous rate of weapons production predicted by the model becomes absurd or impossible. Yet there is another possibility. The justification for the use of a linear differential equations model lies in simplicity and the fact that other nonlinear models can be approximated over a small region by a linear one. When an arms race leaves this region, as would be implied by an unstable model, it might be more realistic to assume that the character of the arms race might change. For example, it is quite plausible that the coefficients in the model might vary depending on the arms levels. The relative significance of the addition of one missile is greater when both sides have 10 than when both sides have 1000. In a similar vein, it is easy--especially after 40 years of US-Soviet arms racing--to imagine a perfectly stable, dynamic equilibrium that is based on a diminishing but still non-zero rate of increase.

Faith in the Richardsonian formulation is not increased by examining historical arms races. Majeski and Jones[16] looked at 12 arms races that have commonly been used by researchers. In most cases, changes in expenditures of one state were only marginally related to those of its opponent and, when they were related, the Richardson specification was not supported. Even allowing for the fact that expenditure levels are an imperfect surrogate for arms levels, this is not encouraging support.

Intrilligator and Brito[17] have investigated the relationship between armament levels and war initiation using an approach that is more sensitive to the contingent effect of arms races and more closely tied to deterrence. They postulate conditions under which a potential attacking side will be deterred, and use these conditions to investigate the effect of changes in armaments levels that might be brought about by any arms race or arms control agreement.

Overall, they reach three conclusions that have a strong deterrence flavor and appear to solve the problem of tying arms decisions to the likelihood of war.

1. An equal arms race from an equal base increases stability. The quantitative, nuclear arms race between the US and Soviet Union reduced the chances that war would occur and provided insurance against the destabilizing potential of qualitative improvement in weapons.
2. The minimum level of stable disarmament that is possible is a function of the potential for technological innovation and treaty verification.
3. Unilateral reductions and unbalanced arms increases can lead to instability and a reduction in deterrence.

This formalizes the contingent effect of arms races on the probability of war that many classical deterrence theorists intuited. Arms races that are balanced decrease the chances that war will occur; arms races that are characterized by differential rates of arms growth will increase the chances of war.

As helpful as their formulation is in explaining why some arms races end in war and others do not, the Brito and Intrilligator treatment does not meet all of the requirements that we would like in a formal theory linking arms races to war. It succeeds in specifying the conditions under which deterrence is sustainable, but it has little to say about the role of strategy, and does not treat arms increases (or decreases) as a decision variable. The last characteristic is more important than it seems. It may be somewhat helpful to tell a state's decisionmakers what part of a decision plane is unstable (i.e., what relative balance of arms stocks is dangerous). However, a point on a plane is not the same as a decision: both the arms levels of two states, and the relative balance between them, are the product of the decisions of both, not just one. If an unbalanced situation exists, decisionmakers of either actor must cope with the dilemma of how to get both states to a more stable point without precipitating war, and whether any strategy they might come up with is worth the costs.

Estimations of what the other side will do in response to their actions are critical to either decision.

One prescription might be that a state interested in decreasing the chances of war would do well to follow a Tit For Tat strategy in which the arms balance is preserved by mimicking the arms behavior of its rival. This is very helpful, but problems arise even when there is **already** balance between the two states. As we have already seen, these can be caused by information uncertainty and misinterpretation. Decisionmakers must not react to nonexistent moves, and the rival state must not overestimate the magnitude or misinterpret the significance of the response. Another problem is that the ability to engage in Tit For Tat is a function of resources. One of the consequences of the incomplete integration of arms races and deterrence theory is that Brito and Intrilligator do not deal with whether or not a state that has fewer resources than its rival is likely to launch a preemptive attack before the arms ratio becomes unbalanced.

When an unbalanced situation exists, the strategies that the two states can be expected to pursue are not clear. The Brito and Intrilligator model makes use of a second threshold which represents the maximum acceptable loss. Although it plays only a small role in their analysis, the idea that there is a level of expected damage which makes even certain victory unattractive is compelling. Historically, it is the key to Swiss deterrence. In terms of arms races such a threshold is important because it places a limit on the effect of resource advantage.

It may have a strategic effect as well. Suppose one state possesses more resources than its rival, and presently enjoys an arms advantage. What strategy should the weaker state follow in this situation? Should it attempt to gradually expand its arms stocks in an effort to reach the threshold where the weapons and resource advantage of the stronger state become irrelevant? What will the more powerful state do? The expectation that this threshold will be reached creates another kind of "window." In this case it is an offensive rather than a defensive window: a last opportunity to expand or to maintain the same level of policy influence, as opposed to a last chance to avoid capitulation or defeat. Instead of preempting inevitable defeat, the state is preempting increased independence and security for its rival. With this in mind, does a decision on the part of the weaker state to step-up arms production increase or decrease the likelihood of war?

Approaches such as that of Bruce Bueno de Mesquita,[18] which focus on expected utility, have not used arms level as a decision variable that is explicitly tied to the probability of war or treated the interaction of states as a game where the success of one state's strategy depends on the strategic behavior of the other. This is not to say that the expected utility school has been silent on the relationship between arms races and war. Morrow[19] employs time series data and indirect measures of risk acceptance and risk aversion to test a number of hypotheses relating the impact of risk attitudes and swings in military superiority on the initiation of conflict. These results are important because they corroborate the importance of transient advantage or "windows." However, further work is still needed to explain the expected utility justification for permitting the existence of such windows. It is not clear why a government or population of voters would be rational in its consideration of the domestic impact of military expenditures, but ignore their impact on the propensity of a rival to initiate hostilities. Is it because the cost of war is underestimated? Or is it because the expected value of satisfying domestic interests is greater than the expected cost of conflict?

Although formal modelers have yet to produce a well-developed theory linking arms race decisions to war, some modest progress has been made while separately exploring the impact of uncertainty on arms races and on deterrence. We have seen that the fact that Tit For Tat is "too ready" to defect to arms increases that might not have taken place--can cause arms spirals. One obvious solution is consistent with the message of the spiral theorists: states should be more forgiving, they should not be provoked by a single defection, or they should respond at a level less than the supposed provocation.

The problem is more complicated if we admit the possibility that we are uncertain about a rival's intentions as well as its arms behavior. At a crude level, how much a state should back away from a strict Tit For Tat response is determined by its assessment of the probability that the rival is motivated by security concerns versus aggressive intent. This can be seen by considering the two archetypical cases. If all opponents are equally aggressive, as naive deterrence theory would have us believe, the cost of departing too greatly from Tit For Tat will be the suggestion of appeasement and the gradual loss of policy influence and, ultimately, security. On the other hand, if states are motivated by the security considerations that lie at the heart of the spiral model, then a modest response can defuse a mutually undesirable arms race before it gets started, or initiate a process that will end an existing race.

Recent work on deterrence by Nalebuff[20] and Powell[21] is helpful in illuminating the effects of uncertainty. One of the important functions of arms behavior is to establish a reputation for strength that will deter aggression and promote policy influence. Shifted to an arms race setting, Nalebuff's discussion of the impact of intervention on reputation suggests that uncertainty can produce a higher rate of building than would exist under perfect information. This higher rate is not sustained because risk averseness inspires an attitude of "better safe than sorry," but because uncertainty provides a state with the opportunity to inflate a rival's perception of capability.

Powell's research on crisis stability also has implications for the arms race/war connection. Although the analogy between crisis escalation and an arms race is imperfect, they have certain characteristics in common: both are driven by a desire for greater policy influence, both involve communicating commitment and capability in a world of uncertainty, and both run the risk of provoking war if one of the participants is convinced that war is inevitable. Using sequential equilibrium models, Powell shows that under very broad assumptions, the chance of a crisis escalating to nuclear war is zero.[22] This is true even when there is an advantage to striking first. For our purposes this suggests that in a MAD world the risk of an arms race resulting in war is similarly small even if there is a first strike advantage or cult of the offensive.

Part of Powell's result stems from the fact that under mutually assured destruction a first strike advantage is worth very little. It basically involves the unenviable opportunity of dying several minutes after a rival. Striking first dominates the outcome of being struck first, but is inferior to **any** other outcome. Not surprisingly, in Powell's model nations always choose to do neither. The more interesting logic driving the finding lies in the argument that no behavior will take place in the escalation bargaining game that is sufficiently aggressive to convince either side that the probability of war exceeds the critical threshold. Because this phenomenon is also a consequence of the costs incurred from a retaliatory strike, this too may seem unremarkable. However, Powell's idea of creating a model that treats the estimate of the probability that the enemy will attack as endogenous is an important innovation. Not only is it responsive to the criticism of the spiral theorists that deterrence models overlook the effect of arms behavior on assessments of intention, but it shows how the cost of aggression (in this case represented by nuclear retaliation) places a limit on what will (or at least should) be inferred. In this way it takes an important step toward uniting the essence of the naive deterrence model and the security dilemma model. What remains to be done is to capitalize on this unification and see what can be said about arms races in which first strike advantages are **not** made irrelevant by retaliatory capacity. Once this assumption is dropped, we can better understand how and why the likelihood that an arms race will end in war varies with defensive capability, uncertainty, and first strike advantage.

The work of Naelbuff and Powell is a beginning, but each makes assumptions about the structure of the game that mask the difficulty of the intentions versus cost question. National policymakers often do not have this luxury. They are not sure whether their counterparts have initiated a weapons program because they are committed to aggression or to increasing their policy influence, because they simply wish to be more secure, or because a domestic constituency demanded it for economic reasons. They do suspect that the motives of their rivals make a difference in what their response should be. A situation of mutually assured destruction makes this problem somewhat simpler because it can ameliorate the effect of modest arms advantages on the probability of total war. Yet there are still difficulties at the level of extended deterrence--will an arms advantage promote military adventurism at the margin?--and the lurking problem of a breakout from MAD.

Conclusion

These brief portraits of the state of deterrence theory in two areas reveal a number of common limitations. At present we have only begun to understand how deterrence actions interact with assessments of intentions. We know something about the impact of reciprocal behavior on this interaction and how it operates in a nuclear context, but there is still a long way to go before the Gordian Knot of prevention/provocation is cut. It is possible that formal theory cannot tell us anything very specific because such behavior is consistent with a wide range of preferences. It is also possible that any inference is treacherous because it is unreasonable to assume that decisionmakers will behave in a fashion consistent with elaborate equilibrium calculations (this would doubtless be the position of critics of rational choice). Yet it is almost certainly an exercise that is worth undertaking.

There are a variety of other issues that also remain unresolved. Sequential equilibrium models are useful tools, but they require some assumptions of convenience about belief systems, stopping points, and updating rules that may be playing a large role in some of their more provocative implications. Similarly, our notions about the nature of credibility are still very crude. The frequency with which extremal solutions (e.g., announce that you will build up your arms supply at the maximum rate for the rest of time if the other side increases arms beyond a certain threshold) are found dominant, raises doubts about the soundness of the whole approach. If the rival state believes such an extreme threat, it will provide a powerful disincentive, but do we trust the claim that it will?

It is also obvious that theoretical weaknesses are constantly compounded by measurement problems. Rational deterrence theory cannot tell us how much a particular benefit or cost is worth to a rival government, its propensity to take risks, its level of uncertainty, the consequences of a leadership change, or the domestic costs of initiating--or not initiating--a conventional war. This information must come from intelligence sources or a combination of intelligence sources and other theories, and it is often absent or unreliable.

Deterrence theorists become understandably frustrated when their theory is blamed for what they view as an intelligence or information failure. It is not, they argue, their responsibility to tell policymakers whether Germany is being run by a Kaiser Wilhelm or a Hitler. Economists are not blamed for needing good data on prices or wages. Critics respond by charging that a theory that demands information that is unobtainable or consistently misperceived by contemporary decisionmakers is not much of a theory.

Only time and experience will resolve this debate. The availability and accuracy of information is likely to vary a great deal across contexts, and neither the deterrence community nor its critics is a good judge of the limits of intelligence and model building in all of these areas.

Notes

1. Paul Huth and Bruce Russett, "Testing Deterrence theory," *World Politics* 32 (1990), p. 477.
2. Richard Ned Lebow, and Janice Gross Stein, "Deterrence: The Elusive Dependent Variable," *World Politics* 32 (1990), p. 354.
3. Huth and Russett, "Testing Deterrence Theory," p. 480.
4. Jack L. Snyder, *The Ideology of the Offensive* (Ithaca, NY: Cornell University Press, 1985).
5. Richard Ned Lebow and Janice Stein, "Beyond Deterrence: Building Better Theory," *Journal of Social Issues* 43 (1987), p. 14.
6. P. Huth, *Extended Deterrence and the Prevention of War* (New Haven, CT: Yale University Press, 1988), p. 204.
7. Huth, *Extended Deterrence*, p. 204.
8. Huth, *Extended Deterrence*, p. 79.
9. Lebow and Stein, "Beyond Deterrence," p. 23.
10. Lebow and Stein, "Beyond Deterrence."
11. George W. Downs and and David M. Rocke, *Tacit Bargaining, Arms Races, and Arms Control* (Ann Arbor: University of Michigan Press, c1990).
12. Paul Diehl, "Arms Races and Escalation: A Closer Look," *Journal of Peace Research* 22 (1983), pp. 249-259.
13. Paul Diehl and Jean Kingston, "Messenger or Message?: Military Buildups and the Initiation of Conflicts," *Journal of Politics* 49 (1987), pp. 801-813.
14. Lewis Fry Richardson, *The Statistics of Deadly Quarrels* (Chicago: Quadrangle Press, 1960).
15. Mobada Simaan and J.B. Cruz, Jr., "Formulation of Richardson's Model of Arms Race from a Differential Game Viewpoint," *Review of Economic Studies* 42 (1975), pp. 67-77.
16. Stephen J. Majeski and David L. Jones, "Arms Race Modelling," *Journal of Conflict Resolution* 25 (1981), pp. 259-288.
17. Dagobert L. Brito and Michael D. Intriligator, "Uncertainty and the Stolidity of the Armaments Race," *Annals of Economic Social Measurement* 3 (1976), pp. 279-292; D. Brito and M. Intriligator, "Formal Models of Arms Races," *Journal of Peace Science* 2 (1976), pp. 77-88; D. Brito and M. Intriligator, "Can Arms Races Lead to

the Outbreak of War?" *Journal of Conflict Resolution* 28 (1984), pp. 63-84.
18.   Bruce Bueno de Mesquita, *The War Trap* (New Haven, CT: Yale University Press, 1981; 1984).
19.   J. Morrow, "A Twist of Truth" (1984). Paper presented at the annual meeting of the American Political Science Association.
20.   Barry Nalebuff, "Rational Deterrence in an Imperfect World," *World Politics* 43 (1990), pp. 313-335.
21.   Robert Powell, *Nuclear Deterrence Theory: The Search for Credibility* (New York: Cambridge University Press, 1989).
22.   *Ibid.*, chs. 5&6.

Part III

Middle Eastern Application

7. Arab Rationality and Deterrence

Gabriel Ben-Dor

A great many countries in practice base their security policies on the idea of deterrence--a concept so powerful in its explanatory logic that one is naturally attracted to its study. Yet most, if not all, the assumptions of a successful environment for deterrence seem lacking in the Middle East, where there is a problem of intercultural communications, and many national interests and policies are not easily amenable to reassurance.

Nevertheless, Arab political culture is not inherently irrational in any meaningful sense of the term.[1] In Arab politics there is calculation of cost and benefit as much as in any other type of political system. True, in the early days of Islam one could find a more disjointed link between cause and effect than in other cultures, due to the attribution of divine intervention in every single human act. But I would argue this does not prevail today in the political culture of Arabs or, for that matter, of other Muslim states.

There is perhaps one exception which should qualify this statement: the conception of radical Shi'ites strongly influenced by the belief in afterlife, and the rewards of martyrdom. This is not by definition irrational, but it leads to a political calculus difficult for any outsider to understand, and causes practical obstacles, for instance in fighting individual Shi'ite terrorism. One hastens to point out, however, that even this fanaticism does not exist on the macro level of states. The one radical Shi'ite regime in power, Iran, has not shown any inclination to be a crazy state, to use a term borrowed from Yehezkel Dror. Hence the conclusion that political rationality does exist in Arab politics.

Moreover, it is difficult to generalize about the Arab world at large, because of the great variations within the Arab state system. The brand of politics practiced in Egypt is radically different from the one practiced in Iraq and Syria, owing to historical, geographic and ethnic variables. In fact, the differences among the various Arab countries are so large as to make them appear as great as the ones between Arabs and non-Arabs. This is very important to bear in mind when attempting to develop a set of generalizations that have a value for the Middle East at large.

Nevertheless, practically all Arab regimes have something in common, and this is their style of politics, which is extremely power-oriented. Historically, practically all Arab rulers have reached power by the threat or use of force. And they retain power thanks to their ability to manipulate its components, physical and psychological. Consequently, Arab politicians have a virtual obsession with power. In other words, a main preoccupation is the survival of the **regime**, which at times includes the **personal** survival of the ruler. In practice this means that any outside military threat aimed at the welfare of the population per se stands to be less effective and less deterrent than the general theoretical literature on deterrence assumes. Arab rulers have other priorities; moreover, the pressure of public opinion on them to avoid external confrontations is not great, given the absence of an open democratic system.

It follows that if deterrence is to work in an Arab context, then it has to be both immediate and direct. Injury will have to be inflicted not just on values dear to the country as such, but on values cherished by the ruling elite, and most likely on the existence in power of the ruling elite itself. This means that the would be deterrer of Arabs must make important distinctions among the various countries. Whether sociological (Egypt), geographic (Iraq), or ethnic (Syria), such a differentiation allows an outsider to identify the foundations of the ruling elite and then to threaten them in order to allow for deterrence to work. Many experts feel that all the damage inflicted on the Egyptian economy in 1969-70 had much less of an effect than the threat to the Third Army in 1973. Since the latter was based on an officer corps consisting of the sons of the ruling elite, their encirclement by Israel's counteroffensive for the first time introduced a direct immediate threat to the lives and welfare of the ruling families. Similarly, many pundits are convinced that Saddam Hussein's willingness to refrain from the use of chemical weapons in the recent Gulf War, and his relatively mild treatment of western prisoners of war, had to do above all with his double fear that any excess would not only have brought about the literal downfall of his regime, but also would have guaranteed personal danger, possibly even trial and execution for war crimes. In my opinion this threat from Washington and London was taken most seriously in Baghdad, and there is a profound lesson to be learned from this.

Of course, such threats are difficult to articulate and to communicate, and not only in terms of the value systems of the western countries, or Israel. There are authentic difficulties of intercultural communications.[2] But while such difficulties are pointed out in the deterrence literature, in the case of the Arab world the problems are that much more acute, due to a culture which attributes immense importance to verbal matters in general, and those involving matters of shame and honor in particular.

These cultural difficulties are exacerbated because there is no continuous and orderly interaction between Arabs and Israelis. Much of the information they obtain about each other contains gross fallacies due to faulty channels of communication that are nonrepresentative, such as oppressed minorities or random individuals. This fragmented system of communications leads to an inability by one side to understand the values of the other, or to interpret its intentions, especially in the light of the stereotypes that characterize the demonology of Israel in the Arab political tradition. This has profound implications for the problematique of deterrence when it comes to the Arab world, particularly for Israel.

This point may be fully appreciated only in the light of the special place that Israel occupies in the Arab political mind in general. It is no secret that Israel is a convenient, and in some sense also logical, explanation of Arab technological backwardness. It is at the very least a constant reminder to the Arabs of their inability to overcome most challenges of modernization. Therefore, they still find it most difficult to accept the existence of Israel. It is easy to imagine the Arab predicament, therefore, when the Arabs are asked not only to accept Israel, but to come to terms with the fact--actual or potential--that Israel possesses sufficient power to prevent them from achieving goals which are desired by them as a matter of course, solely on account of the ability of Israel to inflict unacceptable damage on them. All this is magnified by the glaring asymmetry in tangible power resources between Israel and the Arabs.

This point, too, is critically important. After all, in order to make deterrence credible in the long run, it is necessary not only to look at the actual order of battle, however defined, but also at the potential inherent in the resources of the parties concerned. It is indeed very difficult to accept the long-term advantage of a party which is outmanned, outgunned and outsized in terms of manpower, natural resources, territory, and every other quantifiable component of potential force. Given this blatant lack of symmetry between Israel and its Arab adversaries throughout the past five decades--something that no computerized simulation would come to terms with either--it is no wonder that the Arabs tend to resort to demonological explanations of Israel's ability to inflict so much damage on them; or else that the temporariness of this situation is assumed, hence the Crusader theory. In either case, the conditions for stable deterrence are lacking.

Janice Stein has argued that deterrence is most likely to succeed when the adversaries are motivated largely by the prospect of gain. The evidence also suggests that deterrence is more likely to succeed when an adversary has the political and strategic freedom to exercise restraint, is not misled by grossly distorted assessment of the political-military situation, and is vulnerable to the kinds of threats a deterrer is capable of making.

The timing of deterrence may also be important. The effectiveness of deterrence is likely to be enhanced if it is used early, before an adversary becomes committed to a use of force or becomes correspondingly insensitive to warnings and threat. Insofar as these strategic, political and psychological conditions go unfulfilled, deterrence is increasingly likely to become ineffective, irrelevant, or even provocative. How well this argument applies to the Arab-Israeli situation is seen in the belated warnings by Jerusalem to Damascus on the eve of the 1967 war. Rather than deterring the Arabs, they aggravated the conflict, escalating it to the point of explosion.

Unfortunately, many of the same factors which make deterrence such a difficult proposition in the Arab-Israeli context make reassurance almost equally hard to implement. Demonology does not allow for a true picture of Israel to filter through to Arab decisionmakers. Again, the nature of the Arab regimes and the need-oriented character of their leaders create situations when neither deterrence nor reassurance can cancel their propensity for high risk-taking in order to have a round of fighting--with that single exception of risk to the survival of the regime itself and its leaders. Hence, threats to the latter, which may nullify basic asymmetry, possess greater credibility. An example of this is a subject outside the scope of this paper; namely Arab perceptions of Israel's nuclear capability. It appears to have been central in helping shape the evolving perceptions of one key Arab country, Egypt, during the 1960s and 1970s.

From the history of the conflict between the Arab countries and Israel one gets the strong impression that Arabs find it difficult to accept the very concept of Israeli deterrence. They find it much easier to accept the existence of outside powers bolstering the strength of Israel, as this does not raise the problems of shame, asymmetry or demonology. Hence, an American policy of deterring the Arabs from attacking Israel is something they find much more convenient to live with than the force of Israel itself. Of course, not only does this raise all the theoretical problems associated with the concept of "extended deterrence," but it also raises questions of credibility from the Israeli point of view, and it is certainly not an attractive long-term proposition. Nevertheless, the idea of "delegating deterrence" is one that cannot be dismissed in light of the realities of the Middle East.

This notion of the possible delegation of the deterrence function also has to do with the possible delegation of a message delivery function in the imperfect, indirect system of communications between the adversaries. Granted not only the lack of systemic and orderly avenues of communication, but also cultural barriers which bring about endless misunderstandings even once dependable communications are established, it may well make good sense to look for a credible mediator for the transmission of messages of deterrence. This, if for no better reason than in order to bring about some congruence between the power that is needed to back up deterrence on the one hand, and the power that may be possessed by the mediator on the other. Or to put it differently: while the acceptance of a threatening message from Israel may not be a viable option for certain Arab leaders given not only the asymmetry but also the demonology we have already alluded to, it may be possible to avoid a situation of shame if the message is delivered by a power acknowledged on the Arab side as authentically strong.

Of course, this stratagem must take into account subtle and not so subtle differences between the various Arab state actors. In a country like Egypt which has a relatively long tradition of stateness as well as a legacy of direct negotiations with Israel, the entire system of communications is much easier to manage. Also, Egypt possesses a natural center as well as limited and well-defined areas in which the wealth and the power of the country are concentrated, but also highly vulnerable. In this sense Egypt constitutes a good target for deterrence.

On the other hand, if we take two examples at the other extreme, both Syria and Iraq not only lack traditions of stateness as well as well-managed negotiations with Israel (this is, of course, much more true of Iraq than of Syria), but they also lack the kind of single center that Egypt possesses. Their centers of power and production are diffuse, and therefore difficult to threaten, notwithstanding the importance of Damascus for Syria and Baghdad for Iraq. Hence, we see yet again that in many ways it makes little sense to speak of the Arab world as a monolithic entity for purposes of analysis; rather, we must make distinctions whenever and wherever appropriate.

Yet another theoretical postulate is that no matter how illegitimate a regime may have been when it came into being, the longer the ruler stays in power, the more likely he is to gain a greater degree of respectability. Along with this comes a lower propensity for risk-taking and adventurousness; hence the easier it will be to deter him by using a rational calculus. On the other hand, it should be borne in mind that both Sadat and Asad decided to take a very high risk in 1973 after they had long since consolidated their hold on power, deciding that they could nonetheless afford a measure of threat to their power precisely because they felt so secure. It is not at all certain that Syria at the time was driven by necessity to war with Israel. Rather, conceivably it may have been motivated more by opportunity--to regain the Golan, to defeat Israel, to dominate Arab politics; this, plus the fact that its senior ally, Egypt, was being compelled to war by need. That Asad could afford to join in the enterprise knowing full well the inherent risks is explainable in light of the confidence he felt about the stability and future prospects of his regime. It is also true that since 1973 Asad has shown great patience vis-a-vis the problem of the Golan Heights, and has been in no hurry to undertake military operations in the last 20 years, on the grounds that the opportune moment has not yet come. This, too, can be attributed to the confidence he feels about the survivability of his Alawite regime, which at present does not require bold or desperate measures to prove its ideological zeal and steadfastness against Israel.

The example of Saddam Hussein in Iraq, on the other hand, lends the thesis less support. Saddam's long experience with power, at least as of 1992, has not encouraged him toward a more moderate approach to risk-taking; if anything, perhaps the opposite is true. In the two Gulf wars he precipitated, Saddam has proven himself willing to gamble for very large stakes, each time trading away gains from previous rounds in order to improve his odds in the newest gamble.

Therefore, it is difficult to develop a general theoretical argument around this thesis. One must factor in such intervening variables as the personality, socialization and operational code of each leader, for these apparently make a decisive difference. In certain instances deterrence may collapse when leaders are compelled by excessive need (as was Sadat in 1973); or when leaders are driven by ambition and personality to such an extent that they neglect the possibility of their country suffering severe punishment. But then in the light of such possibilities one may well query whether deterrence stands any prospect of success in the first place.

A major problem common to deterrence and reassurance is the nature of the highly verbal Arab political culture. Can one really and effectively deter a leader who regards the prospect of confrontation between his Third World army, on the one hand, and a genuine superpower, on the other, as "the mother of all battles?" What prospects are there for dissuading a leader who takes literally an oblique hint that the superpower will not intervene in border squabbles of Arab neighbors, interpreting it as carte blanche to undertake an Anschluss in a blitzkrieg?

This is one of the most fundamental problems to be faced. The delivering and deciphering of messages constitute the heart of the process of deterrence; and they are equally important, if not more so, for the purposes of reassurance as well. Moreover, if we wish to apply principles of rationality to deterrence, then the calculus of rationality must be articulated verbally. Herein lies the critical importance of how words are used, and to what extent they are reliable as vehicles of communicating messages that can either deter or reassure--taken seriously and understood more or less in the way intended by the originator of the message.

The question of verbal communications in deterrence and reassurance is more complicated by an Arab world undergoing rapid processes of modernization. In practice this means that traditional modes of verbal expression will have been radically changed among members of the younger generation who are increasingly accustomed to western modes of expression. Even if in theory we were able to work out a way to understand all the subtleties and nuances of Arab verbal culture, we would then face the insoluble problem of differential rates of modernization among the various political elites.

There is little hope of compiling a dictionary or vocabulary that would allow us to translate Arab verbal responses and expressions to a language more commonly used and understood in international politics. What remains to be done by those who would venture to use strategies of deterrence against Arabs is a determined effort to use deterrence terminology that is clear, consistent and unambiguous, at the same time taking into account the sensitivity of Arab culture to honor and shame. Set aside here is inter-Arab deterrence--a fascinating subject in its own right, but which has received so little scholarly attention that in my opinion we are unable at the moment to learn anything of general scholarly value about it; not to mention that the problems of communication are of an entirely different order of magnitude.

It follows that a secret diplomacy for delivering messages of deterrence is more likely to succeed than the open and public mode. This allows on the one hand a directness which may help cut across the ambiguities that give rise to dangerous misunderstandings, while on the other hand avoiding shame or disgrace if the deterrence threat is brutal.

In any case, there seems every reason to caution strongly against attempts to try to outdo the Arabs in verbal subtleties, as tried by Ms. Glaspie on the eve of the Iraqi invasion of Kuwait. Not only does such an approach lead to misunderstandings, as in the case just quoted, but it also makes it difficult at a later time to communicate a clear and consistent set of messages which may allow a coherent doctrine of deterrence to be articulated, communicated and understood. This seems to hold true for Israelis and western powers, as well as for Turkey and Iran which also deal extensively with major Arab powers.

When attempting to summarize the case of the Arab world, one should bear in mind that the basic assumptions of rationality upon which the classic approach to deterrence is based have been thoroughly challenged in the light of recently available empirical evidence. It is not easy, for example, to dismiss the argument of Lebow and Stein, for whom deterrence theories presuppose incorrectly that leaders are (1) instrumentally rational, (2) risk-prone gain maximizers, (3) free of domestic constraints, and (4) able correctly to identify themselves as defenders or challengers. All of these core assumptions are unrealistic and contradicted by empirical evidence. Lebow and Stein go on to conclude that "If rational deterrence theories are to be useful as empirical theories, they must open their fundamental assumptions and behavioral implications to empirical evaluation, not protect or shield them from scrutiny."[3]

Quite simply, the empirical evidence found in the study of Arab politics does not support the assumption of classic and pure rational deterrence theory based on data and experience collected elsewhere. In fact, the Arab cases pose an even greater challenge, not because there is anything inherently less rational in Arab political culture or behavior, but because the patterns of Arab political development are such as to make the evolving regimes even more bound by domestic constraint, their leaders even more driven by need than opportunity, and their rhetoric even more difficult and ambiguous as a medium of communication, thus lessening access to "perfect" as well as other kinds of information even more than in other parts of the globe.

Unfortunately, the very same difficulties of communication and interpretation of messages (compounded by the complexity of interaction with a regional actor which has been shaped by entirely different cultural experiences) also render Stein's alternative concept, that of "reassurance" almost as difficult to apply as deterrence. Still, in purely logical-theoretical terms, in the long run the rationality of reassurance may be easier to accept than the rationality of deterrence. At the same time, the fact remains that historically the core of Israel's security doctrine--which by definition is the principal Israeli answer to the threats posed by potential Arab hostility--is precisely deterrence. This, too, is an empirical fact of Middle East life, as is the rationality shown by the major Arab power which Israel managed to deter more than any other, Egypt, and now seeks to reassure. Rather than mere coincidence, the Israeli-Egyptian dialogue is further evidence that deterrence and reassurance are two sides of the same coin. Only an environment which allows the one can also allow the other.

Can Arabs be deterred rationally? Clearly, in many cases they can, in some significant others they cannot. And not because their leaders are less rational than their counterparts in other countries. Instead, the shortcomings of western and superpower rational theory models of deterrence are that much more glaring because of the sharp contrast that the Arab political environment presents.

To the extent that any power dealing with the Arabs intends to utilize strategies of deterrence systematically over some length of time, it must be able to define, demonstrate and communicate its own set of rational principles in order to make sure there is a consistent, accurate Arab perception. For this alone allows hope for deterrence to be successful.

Notes

1.   See Gabriel Ben-Dor, "Political Culture Approach to Middle East Politics," *International Journal of Middle East Studies*, January 1976; and Ben-Dor, *State and Conflict in the Middle East* (New York: Praeger, 1983).
2.   See Gabriel Ben-Dor, "Miscommunication and Fallacies in the Arab-Israeli Conflict," in Nissan Oren, ed., *Images and Reality in World Politics* (forthcoming).
3.   Ned Lebow and Janice Gross Stein, "Rational Deterrence Theory: I Think, Therefore I Deter," *World Politics* (January 1989), p. 223.

8. Deterrence Experience in the Arab-Israel Conflict

Yair Evron

My purpose here is to discuss some aspects of the deterrence relationship between Israel and its Arab opponents. Before detailing these specific aspects, it should be noted that the political-strategic history of the modern Middle East is replete with both successful and failed exercises in deterrence, coercion and compellence,[1] whether between Arab states and Israel or among the Arab states themselves. The richness of this experience is due to the prevalence of inter-state conflicts in the region. In the Arab-Israeli context, each side has applied strategies of deterrence at different times or simultaneously. However, being in most cases the status quo power, Israel is found to have applied such strategies both more often and more saliently. For this reason, Israeli deterrence posture serves as the main focus of discussion in the following chapter.

Generally speaking, deterrence is a strategy designed to stabilize strategic relationships, its main objective being to constrain military behavior and preempt escalations to war. It is therefore one of the principal strategies of conflict and crisis management. Indeed, in very fierce conflicts that are either absolute or approximate zero-sum games and where the only shared interest of the opponents is a common fear of the costs of war, deterrence is **the** most important management strategy. In conflicts where other common or coincidental interests exist, deterrence should be complemented by other strategies of conflict and crisis management mediated through diplomacy.

Deterrence is primarily designed to achieve strategic stability. Yet exclusive reliance on it for long periods of time in situations where diplomacy and political compromise could constrain or even resolve conflicts may in fact aggravate the situation. This is because deterrence never deals with the basic sources of a conflict and therefore is only a management strategy of limited duration. Indeed, as we shall see below, when politics are divorced from military deterrence, prospects for the latter's success actually diminish.

One distinction developed in deterrence literature that is directly relevant to our discussion differentiates between "immediate" or "specific" deterrence and "general" deterrence. Specific deterrence refers to a situation in which the deterrer perceives a potential **specific** action by the challenger intended to change the status quo, and so issues a deterring threat. General deterrence denotes the buildup of military capabilities by the deterrer for the ongoing deterrence of a whole range of potential moves by the challenger. General deterrence, therefore, is close to some aspects of the notion of "balance of power." It is, however, a much more limited concept. This distinction is inspired by a formulation suggested by Morgan,[2] who distinguished between "immediate" or "pure" deterrence, which refers to an imminent planned action by the challenger, and "general" deterrence. My definition of "specific" deterrence includes immediate deterrence, but in addition encompasses other specific deterrence threats which might also pertain to potential future challenging acts. The obvious case of such threats are definitions of casus belli.

The Israeli Deterrence Posture[3]--
A Brief Historical Account[4]

Needless to say, deterrence forms but one aspect of the overall Israeli strategic posture. No strategic posture in a conventional environment can depend exclusively, or even mainly, on deterrence. Since the end of its War of Independence in 1948, Israel has sought to deter three different types of military threats: low level violence such as infiltration and sabotage actions by irregulars, small-scale military operations carried out by regular forces, and full-scale wars.

Deterrence of low level violence. Infiltration has been a hindrance to Israel almost since the end of the 1948 War, and in the first years after independence its initial military response to such acts was spasmodic. When the scope of terrorist infiltration widened in the first half of the '50s, by late 1953, and more so from 1954 on, Israel developed a new, more comprehensive strategy of response, identified primarily with the then IDF chief of staff, General Moshe Dayan.[5]

The new strategy had several objectives. The first objective could be defined as 'third party (or indirect) deterrence'[6] in which military pressure was applied on the Arab governments from whose territories the infiltration took place. The idea was that such military pressure, applied through military attacks on military targets and on villages where the infiltrators were based, would compel the respective Arab governments to control the infiltrators and curtail hostile actions, each action serving as a signal that further 'punishment' was imminent unless the infiltration ceased. Secondly, the strategy involved elements of 'compellence,' such as the attempts to force Arab acceptance of Israeli political conditions which until the 1967 war, included acceptance of the 1949 territorial status quo and the signing of a peace treaty. A third objective was escalatory in nature. It seems that some Israeli decisionmakers, in particular Dayan, were hoping that the dynamics of retaliation and counter-retaliation would ultimately lead to a general war. This objective became more salient during 1955-1956 in relation to Egypt. Needless to say, this escalatory function and, to a lesser extent, the function of 'compellence,' if accurately perceived by the target state, exert an influence on the latter that is diametrically opposed to the effect of deterrence.

The strategy of "third party deterrence" was partly successful when applied to Jordan against Jordanian-based infiltrators in the '50s and again in the mid-'60s. The same policy was largely ineffective against Jordan in the late '60s, and against Lebanon since the early '70s. The use of the strategy against Egypt in 1955-1956, rather than deterring infiltration, led to a vicious cycle of actions and counteractions that culminated in the 1956 War.[7] A similar though not identical process took place along the Israeli-Syrian border in 1964-1967.

Deterrence against full-scale war. The most important element in Israeli deterrence strategy has been to frustrate the initiation of a regular war by any Arab state or coalition of states.

In analyzing this aspect of Israeli deterrence, account must be made of two important complexes: the actual deterrence posture, which is the outcome of both military capabilities and doctrine, and public references by decisionmakers; and secondly, the success or failure of deterrence.

The success or failure of deterrence is difficult to prove. For a deterrence threat to succeed, the following process must ensue: the challenger contemplates a military action which threatens a deterrer's interest; the deterrer is aware of this contemplated action and issues a deterrence threat; the threat is perceived by the challenger; the challenger reconsiders the cost/benefit balance of his intended action, integrating the deterrence threat into his calculations; and finally, the challenger decides to abandon his intended action in view of the deterrence threat. To state it differently, successful deterrence means that were it not for the threat, the challenger would have decided to proceed with the intended action.

Recorded evidence for all these stages is not easily accessible. The analytic difficulties increase when one has to rely on public pronouncements by the challenger's decisionmakers explaining their policy choices and decisions. Therefore, their actual actions or inactions may be a better guide.

Since the end of the 1948/49 War, there have been five Arab-Israeli wars: 1956, 1967, 1969/70, 1973 and 1982. Questions of the relevance and of the success or failure of Israeli deterrence will now be considered in regard to 1956, 1967, 1973 and 1982.[8] In terms of the success or failure of general deterrence, the 1969/70 War of Attrition served as a prelude to the 1973 War.

The Israeli deterrence posture 1949-1956 and its relevance to the 1956 war. In the early '50s, the then chief of staff, Yigael Yadin, formulated an **operational** military doctrine, which nonetheless encompassed some central strategic principles.[9] Yadin's doctrine comprised several principles which on the political-strategic level could be seen as fitting a deterrence approach. However, a coherent strategy of deterrence against all-out war had to await the aftermath of the 1956 Sinai campaign.

By late 1954-1955 Israel perceived a new critical threat emanating from the Arab side. For Israel's chief decisionmaker,

Ben-Gurion, the emergence of Nasser as a new, vigorous and apparently unifying leader of the Arab world, constituted a major long-term threat to Israel. According to this perception, once Nasser resolved his relationship with Britain, he would unite the Arab world and lead a major war against Israel.

Notwithstanding Arab rhetoric calling for a "second round" against Israel, it could be argued that until late 1955 the Arab states were in fact almost entirely preoccupied with other sets of problems: domestic issues, the struggle against Britain, and inter-Arab competition. From early 1955, Egypt became more actively involved in the conflict with Israel, due first to the process of escalation along the Israeli border, and secondly to the accelerated arms race. It is not clear, however, to what extent Nasser was considering initiating hostilities. In any case other Arab states, primarily Iraq and Jordan, belonged to a different Arab bloc and were not allied to Egypt. Indeed, rather than contemplating war against Israel, Iraqi leaders would have welcomed a military defeat for Nasser, even at the hands of Israel.

However, what counted most in the ensuing escalation were the Israeli perceptions. The Israeli response to its perceived threat was not to adopt a deterrence strategy, but rather to seek an opportunity for a military action to destroy Egyptian arms, and if possible to undermine Nasser's regime.

Consequently, the period between 1954-1956 marked a change in the Israeli politico-strategic orientation. Initially, through the strategy of retaliation described above, there was an attempt to **compel** the Arab side and primarily Egypt to accept the territorial status quo and the Israeli conditions for a peace settlement. Nuances in the Israeli retaliatory strategy suggested that some of the leadership went beyond compellence and would have welcomed a process of military escalation leading to a full-scale war. With the acceleration of the arms race from late 1955, the trend toward a preventive war was set in motion. The emphasis on fighting a war, coupled with notions about the use of force for political compellence, undercut any development of a deterrence strategy.[10]

Israel did not apply a strategy of deterrence against Egypt in 1955-1956, but rather a strategy of escalation, and it was the party that ultimately launched the attack. Thus, in Ben-Gurion's view, the 1956 war was a preventive war.[11] The question of the success or failure of Israel's deterrence therefore does not arise at all in relation to the 1956 War, because deterrence was in fact irrelevant.

The Israeli deterrence posture 1956-1967 and its effectiveness. In the wake of the 1956 War, changes were introduced into the Israeli politico-strategic approach, resulting from a two-fold realization: (a) of the tremendous political constraints on any Israeli military victory, and (b) that military victory would not secure Arab acceptance of the political and territorial status quo. On the other hand, there was general pessimism as to the possibility of a political breakthrough in relations with the Arabs, and especially with Egypt. An alternative strategy seemed to be the avoidance of war primarily through deterrence. Indeed, a more elaborate emphasis on conventional deterrence emerged in the late 1950s and early 1960s, and was especially apparent after 1963 when Rabin became chief of staff, and Eshkol, prime minister.

Due to significant demographic, geographic and economic constraints operating on Israel, it has had to rely primarily on a reserve army. This reliance has dictated its endorsement of an offensive operational doctrine. Thus, on the one hand, Israel moved toward an emphasis on strategy of defense and deterrence, while on the other hand, it has had to rely on an offensive posture at the operational level. The link between the strategic and the operational level came in the "specific deterrence" system of casus belli. Among the casus belli were:

1. The closure of the Straits of Tiran to Israeli shipping, which became the most 'official' of all Israeli casus belli.
2. The introduction of foreign Arab troops into Jordan.
3. A major concentration of Arab forces close to the vital areas of Israel, referring primarily to the massing of Egyptian forces in the Sinai.

Clearly, the massing of large concentrations of Egyptian forces near the international border, or of hostile forces in the Jordan 'bulge' in the West Bank, were the most critical. Such eventualities would

103

threaten the vital areas of Israel, especially in the case of a surprise attack. Hence, from the point of view of Israel's real **strategic** interests, the probability of an Israeli military reaction in the form of a preemptive strike would have been very high.

During this period 1957-1967, the Israeli-Egyptian strategic relationship was remarkably stable, due to a convergence of several factors. All relate to the three balances that affect the calculations of the challenger: the balances of perceived military power, political interests and resolve. These balances should be viewed within the broad political situation prevailing in the Middle East at the time.

To begin with, the balance of military power favored Israel. Moreover, the main Arab opponents, Egypt and Syria, perceived the military balance as such, and did not believe in their capacity to completely defeat Israel on the battlefield.[12] It is reasonable to assume that until the 1967 crisis, Egypt also was not entirely confident in its capacity to defend Sinai against an Israeli attack. The 1956 war, while ending with an Egyptian political success, demonstrated inherent Egyptian military weakness.

In terms of the balance of political interests, it seems most probable that the leading Arab countries did not perceive the Israel-Arab conflict and the resolution of the Palestinian problem as being the most urgent of their priorities. Despite their extreme anti-Israel rhetoric, there can be no other explanation of their all-engrossing involvement in the fierce inter-Arab competition, which accelerated in the first half of the 1960s. At that time, radical and conservative states were in conflict, and the radical camp itself was deeply divided. The Yemen War absorbed much Saudi and Egyptian energy, while Syria and Iraq were busy nibbling at Nasser's regional influence. Leadership of the Arab world appeared to be much more important than a war against Israel. The combination of the first two balances, and the ways in which they were perceived, contributed to the emergence of a credible posture of Israeli deterrence by denial.

One can infer from Egyptian behavior that generally speaking, during the period 1957-1967 Egypt viewed Israeli readiness to escalate hostilities as quite high. This was the source of Egypt's concern over Syrian plans for diversion of the Jordan river. It viewed seriously the dangers involved in a violation of the two Israeli casus belli that were related to its own behavior, that is, the massing of Egyptian forces in the eastern part of Sinai and the closure of the Straits of Tiran. Egypt clearly understood the major risk Israel would face were Egyptian forces to enter the Sinai and be deployed massively along the Israeli border; as a result, it refrained from deploying sizeable forces in the Sinai. Indeed, Sinai was to a large extent demilitarized de facto during 1957-1967. Egypt was also aware of the Israeli strategic doctrine calling for a preemptive strike in the case of a violation of that particular casus belli. In short, Israeli specific and general deterrence against Egypt was successful during this period.

However, when escalation along the Israeli-Syrian border reached threatening dimensions in 1967, Egypt decided to send forces into Sinai in May 1967, as a move designed to deter Israel from initiating an attack on Syria. Whether or not Israel planned such an attack is not important in this context. What is important were the Egyptian leaders' perceptions at the time, in that they believed an Israeli attack on Syria was probable.[13] In addition, Nasser probably believed that this move might improve the Egyptian position in the Arab world, which had suffered due to the Yemen War and inter-Arab competition.

Thus the Egyptian move itself constituted an act of deterrence, and as such did not point to the failure of Israeli **general** deterrence. It did demonstrate a partial failure in regard to **specific** deterrence, viz. a violation of one casus belli concerning the massing of Egyptian troops in the Sinai desert.

The process of the 1967 crisis suggests that, beyond calculations relevant to the balance of interests, military power and resolve, stable deterrence can be maintained provided both sides are aware of the nature of their opponent's general **and** specific deterrence postures, and that both sides are careful not to adopt additional deterrence measures which might violate an opponent's tolerance thresholds concerning which it has already issued deterrence threats. The Israeli escalatory moves along the Syrian border, although partially justified by Syrian actions, nevertheless forced Egypt to adopt deterrence moves which violated essential

Israeli tolerance thresholds. The general threat to stability resulting from conflicting deterrence postures, becomes even more ominous when the behavior of the two sides depends to a large extent on a third uncontrollable party, as Syria was at the time.

Once the situation began to escalate, the dynamics of deterrence were replaced by the dynamics of crisis. Egypt went beyond its initial deterrence action and sought to accomplish political objectives. It moved from a purely deterrence posture at the beginning of the crisis, to a deterrence-cum-compellence posture at a later point. In addition to the violation of the two casus belli-- massing of troops and the threatened closure of the Straits of Tiran-- Israel could have expected further Egyptian demands. It might be speculated that even without the change in the Egyptian posture, Israel would have had to preempt because of the threat posed by the massing of Egyptian forces near the international border, and possibly in order to maintain the credibility of its deterrence in regard to specific threats. The change in Egyptian behavior nevertheless added to Israel's feeling of urgency in the crisis. Consequently, Israel attacked.

To summarize, the Egyptians were at first intent on deterrence, but then utilized the crisis for the achievement of political gains. In both these strategies, the underlying approach was **not** to initiate the actual use of force. All this only underlines the basic point concerning the continued effectiveness of the Israeli **general** deterrence posture even during the crisis itself. To state it succinctly: the two countries differed in their approach to the crisis and in their preferred strategic choices. Because of the primacy of strategic considerations, Israel decided to preempt, while Egypt would probably have preferred the management of the crisis (with some political achievement) without resort to military force.

Until 1967, the Israeli strategic doctrine during the '60s was remarkably coherent and internally logical. As such, it created an effective context for successful **general deterrence**. Were it not for a process of escalation with Syria (to which Israel contributed considerably), coupled with intensified competition in the Arab world, Egypt would not have initiated the crisis during which Israeli **specific deterrence** failed. This leads to another observation regarding Israeli deterrence: The system of casus belli and its attendant system of **specific** deterrence could have been more effective. Yet greater efficacy would have required a greater awareness by Israel of the politico-strategic context in which Egypt and Syria were operating. But Israel failed to consider Egyptian tolerance thresholds. Escalating border violence with Syria clearly violated these thresholds. Maintaining strategic stability with Egypt should have dictated more constrained military activity against Syria.

Failure of deterrence: 1967-1973. The overwhelming Israeli victory of 1967 should have bolstered the Israeli deterrence posture in several profound ways. To begin with, the balance of military power was found to be in Israel's favor to a previously unimagined extent. Moreover, this Israeli superiority was perceived as such by the Arab world. In the second place, American political and military backing for Israel during and following the war, seemed to promise that the arms race ensuing after the war would not undermine Israel's demonstrated military superiority. Finally, the new ceasefire borders appeared, at first glance, to further increase the said military gap. (That the new borders did **not** supply additional security was amply demonstrated during the 1973 War). In summary then, the objective and mutually perceived balance of military power should have enhanced the Israeli deterrence posture.[14] That deterrence ultimately failed was not related to the military balance.

In terms of the balance of political interests, a traditional major Israeli misperception persisted. Israel maintained that Arab animosity toward Israel was a constant, and primarily derived from the basic Arab refusal to legitimize Israel. This basic animosity, it was understood, leads to periodic eruptions for which the main, if not exclusive, responsibility lies with the Arabs. Little attention was paid to the fact that the consequences of the 1967 War, that is, the continued Israeli occupation of Egyptian and Syrian territories, transformed the nature of the conflict. The element of grievance, or as it were, the vitality of Egyptian and Syrian interests involved in the liberation of the Sinai and the Golan Heights, far exceeded their traditional commitment to the Palestinian cause. From a general posture of hostility toward Israel, related to notions of general Arab nationalism, there had been a switch to respectively particularist

Egyptian and Syrian vital national interests. These particularist interests were much more important and central for Egypt and Syria respectively, than the traditional Arab reasons for hostility against Israel.

Hence the balance of interests swung in a way that undermined Israeli deterrence. The Egyptian and Syrian motivation to launch a military strike in order to redress their grievance only increased following 1967. Moreover, in the face of Israeli superiority, war was seen by Egypt as a political instrument, with its military outcome less important than its political consequences. Consequently, Israeli general deterrence failed for the first time. The 1969/70 Attrition War and the 1973 War resulted.

Israeli-specific deterrence system in Lebanon.[15] It is within the context of relations with Syria in Lebanon that Israel has developed, since 1976, a complex system of specific deterrence. Here I shall mention only the main features of this system:

1. Beginning in early 1976, Israel and Syria began exchanging signals, mainly through the good offices of the United States, concerning Syrian military intervention in Lebanon and the limits on such intervention. Washington was very active in promoting understandings between the two states in regard to such military activity. In addition, Israel sent other tacit deterrence signals.

2. By March-April of that year, the two states succeeded in working out a system of mutually agreed "red lines" delimiting the scope of the intended Syrian military intervention in Lebanon. Accordingly, Syrian forces penetrated Lebanon toward the end of May, attacking the PLO and Muslim-radical militias. The limits imposed on the intervention by the Israeli deterrence signals related to the geographical area in which the Syrian forces were "allowed" to operate, the size of forces to be involved and the nature of their weapons systems. In general, Syria adhered to these limitations. Of the latter, the most important were the limitations on the operation of the Syrian Air Force in

Lebanese air space, and on the introduction and deployment of air-to-surface missiles.

3. The Israeli-Syrian understandings, and the consequent strategic stability obtaining between these two countries in Lebanon, depended on several factors: First, Israeli recognition of the vitality of Syrian political interests in Lebanon. Israel also recognized that its own political interests in Lebanon were less vital to it than the Syrian interests were to Syria. Secondly, Syria perceived the balance of military power as favoring Israel. Third, the two states realized that possibly they had shared or coincidental interests in Lebanon: the defeat of the PLO and of the Muslim-radical coalition. Finally, the deep involvement of the United States was heavily instrumental in the achievement of these understandings.

In summary, within a special political context, the Israeli system of "specific deterrence" toward Lebanon operated successfully for about six years. Although it broke down because of the Israeli invasion of Lebanon, it was renewed later on in a somewhat different fashion following Israel's withdrawal from Lebanon.

Israeli Conventional Deterrence--
Some Interim Conclusions

To sum up, it seems that the Israeli general conventional deterrence has been highly successful for long periods of time; indeed it failed only in 1973.[16] This failure resulted from critical changes in the levels of Egyptian and Syrian motivation, caused by a raised intensity of political grievance (even then the failure was only partial, since the attackers opted for a limited campaign only). This historical experience demonstrates that had Israel been conscious of the delicate interactions between the balance of military power and the balance of political interests, it might have saved itself both the 1967 and 1973 wars. Moreover, such Israeli understandings of the nuances of deterrence, coupled with a moderate political approach, could further enhance Israel's conventional deterrence. One of the important instruments for this would be the reformulation of an updated system of casus belli, defined in a rational and sophisticated way, and designed to protect only vital security interests. Furthermore, these casus belli should not be perceived by the opponents as violating **their** political and strategic vital interests.

Several generalizations, some theoretical, may be drawn from the deterrence experience outlined here. First, deterrence is indeed a very complex process in which political, strategic and military factors interact; it cannot be reduced to mere assessments of military balances. In multipolar state systems--as is the case in the Middle East--in which there exist several axes of competition, conflict and cooperation, deterrence becomes even more complex. The effectiveness of deterrent threats and deterrent thresholds depends only partly on the direct relationship between challenger and deterrer, and partly on their resonance in other parts of the system.

Second, deterrence theory as it developed primarily in the United States, has emphasized--because of the requirements of extended deterrence--the importance of credibility of commitments and the ways in which commitments are communicated. This also led to focusing on questions of resolve and projection of images of resolve. In the context of Israeli deterrence, on the other hand, it appears that demonstrations of resolve are not required in order to enhance the credibility of Israeli readiness to defend Israel proper or, for that matter, the territories under its occupation. The question of resolve and credibility may become more relevant in the rare cases of extended deterrence (such as defense of the Maronites in Lebanon), which in any event are not critical for Israeli security.

Third, and related to the second generalization, deterrence failures in the Arab-Israeli context were not related to cognitive problems. What undermined deterrence was not irrationality or a problem of communicating commitments.[17] Even the scope of miscalculations was rather limited. Altogether, Arab political leaders demonstrated quite accurate perceptions of the military balance and believed the various deterrence commitments made by Israel. They undertook escalatory moves, either because they were compelled to do so by deep political grievances (as in 1973)[18] or because they were caught up in the dynamics of a crisis and were affected by sets of political considerations beyond those obtaining in their direct relations with Israel (as in 1967).

The Nuclear Component in Israel's Deterrence-- A Brief Reference[19]

It is close to impossible to do justice to this extensive and very complex issue in a brief discussion. A short reference is necessary, however, because it has been increasingly suggested that Israel's assumed nuclear capability has become its main deterrent, or at least a very important component of it, and moreover, that it played an important role in Israel's deterrence in the past. Regarding the latter supposition, however, a careful study of this subject would lead to the conclusion that the assumed Israeli nuclear capability was largely irrelevant to the dynamics of the Arab-Israel conflict.[20] In other words, it did not act either as a deterrent or as an instrument affecting Arab political postures toward Israel. These observations require some elaboration.

Earlier in this paper, I noted the relative successes of the Israeli conventional general deterrence posture. By the early 1970s, however, international reports began suggesting that Israel may already have assembled a small arsenal of nuclear weapons. Did this substitute for conventional deterrence? The answer is clearly negative. Notwithstanding both Israel's explicit conventional capability and its assumed nuclear one, Egypt and Syria launched their attack in 1973. Some observers have suggested the 1973 attack was limited because Arab leaders suspected that Israel already had at that time a nuclear-weapon capability. But there is no evidence for this, and in fact, bearing in mind the Egyptian and Syrian image of superior Israeli conventional capability, which was enhanced many times by the 1967 Israeli victory, the limits they imposed on their own attack were completely explainable by Israel's conventional capability. Indeed, this can also be demonstrated by both the planning and execution of the coordinated Syrian-Egyptian attack.

It should be added that Arab decisionmakers were indeed absolutely correct in their estimates of Israel's conventional superiority (something which Israel also believed in, and correctly so). The war indeed ended in a military reversal for the Arab side.

Once President Sadat chose to reach a peaceful accommodation with Israel and to opt out of war coalitions against it, a glaring light was thrown on Syria's complete inability to initiate war against Israel by itself. It was clear that without Egypt's participation in a war coalition, no major war could be launched. Thus, by any assessment, even on the basis of the conventional balance, Syria was deprived of the military option for a major war, and has remained in that state ever since. Israel's assumed nuclear capability was therefore superfluous in this context. Whether Syria believes it is capable of launching some version of a limited war, especially a stationary one, without unacceptable costs caused by Israel's conventional capability, is a different question. In any event, it is unlikely that Israel's nuclear deterrent is relevant to such an eventuality.

Another question is whether Israel's assumed nuclear capability created a long-term deterrence effect that may have convinced Syria (and other Arab states) to change their basic political attitudes toward it. In this case, deterrence may have turned into a coercive political instrument.[21] We shall briefly discuss here the Syrian position.

It is not clear when Syrian leaders reached the conclusion that Israel very likely possesses nuclear capability. It can be assumed, however, that with Mordechai Vanunu's revelations in late 1986, Damascus became convinced there was a very high probability that Israel had a nuclear arsenal. In a significant speech reacting to these revelations,[22] President Asad insisted that Syria's objectives toward Israel would not change even if Israel had such a capability. He probably was ready then, as indeed he was even before that, to accept a state of nonbelligerency toward Israel in exchange for the return of the Golan. But he continued to regard the basic conflict with Israel, rooted in Ba'athist party ideology, as an eternal one, its final resolution to be accomplished when the Arab world acquired the necessary capability to fight against it.

Thus the perception of an Israeli nuclear capability did not change Asad's basic position. But another development apparently did. The enormous changes in the international system--the end of the Cold War, the decline of the Soviet Union and the emergence of the United States as the single global power--all these, in a process that began in 1988, led Asad to the conclusion that he had to adopt a completely pragmatic approach toward Israel. This led to his decision to join the peace talks.

In summary, then, up to the present, the assumed Israeli nuclear capability has been largely irrelevant to the main political and strategic developments in the conflict. The usefulness of this capability is in providing Israel a measure of rational response against two possible future developments: as an option of "last resort," in case a grand war coalition were to form against Israel and to succeed in defeating its conventional capability; and secondly, in case an Arab state were to acquire a nuclear capability.[23]

Finally, there is the question of deterrence against the use of chemical weapons against Israeli centers of population. This will be briefly discussed in the next section, as it is closely linked to Israeli deterrence during the Gulf crisis and war.

Israeli Deterrence during the Gulf Crisis[24]

Beginning in April 1990, Iraq and Israel conducted a "deterrence dialogue" concerning what Iraq perceived to be the possibility of an Israeli preemptive strike against Iraq's nuclear infrastructure.[25] But following the invasion of Kuwait, this dialogue changed in nature. Iraqi spokesmen tried to link Israel to the Kuwait situation and to turn the evolving crisis into an Arab-Israeli crisis. Clearly, they hoped this would undermine the Arab coalition forming against them.

When the possibility of an international military move against Iraq became more real, Iraqi spokesmen threatened that such a move would result in surface-to-surface missile attacks on Israel. The Iraqi threats were probably designed to achieve two objectives: first, on the political level, to turn the crisis, and possible eventual war, into an Arab-Israeli affair, thus undermining Arab backing for war against

Iraq; and secondly, to deter the United States from initiating the strike against Iraq. This presumably could be achieved if Israel, worried by the Iraqi threats, were to apply pressure on the United States to desist from war.

Israel, for its part, issued deterring counterthreats against Iraq. Israeli spokesmen warned Baghdad that missile attacks would result in extremely severe retribution. The Israeli deterring posture, however, harbored two ambiguities. First, regarding the nature of the Iraqi provocation: it remained unclear exactly what type of provocation would lead to Israeli retaliation. Three different contingencies were mentioned: conventional air and missile strikes; the use of chemical weapons; and the introduction of Iraqi ground forces into Jordan. The second ambiguity involved the nature of the possible reaction: would it take the form of air strikes or ground operations? The scope of retaliation also remained unclear.

Although Israeli spokesmen refrained from mentioning nuclear retaliation, international and some unofficial Israeli observers interpreted the Israeli warnings as referring to this. Whether such retaliation would come as a response to any attack or only to "nonconventional" (meaning chemical) strikes, also remained unclear in these interpretations.

Once the military phase of the crisis actually began, Iraq launched surface-to-surface missiles of the al-Hussein type against Israeli population centers. The clear objective of the attacks was political: namely, to drag Israel into the war and thus disrupt the political and strategic cohesion of the Arab group within the international coalition. In any case, the very launching of the missiles ostensibly demonstrated the failure of Israeli deterrence.

The reason for this apparent failure, however, was that Iraq in fact desired the threatened Israeli retaliation. The Iraqi leadership calculated that Israeli retaliation would serve the declared purpose of disrupting the coalition. Thus, Iraq probably welcomed in the first place the Israeli deterrent threats and was hoping for their implementation. In this sense, Israeli deterrence did not fail, since deterrence was not relevant to Iraq's political and strategic objectives.

The cards indeed were all stacked in Iraq's favor. If Israel retaliated, it was all for the best. If it failed to do so, another Iraqi aim would be accomplished: to demonstrate to Arab publics its ability to strike at Israel without the latter responding.

Although Iraq did not refrain from launching missiles against Israel, it did avoid using chemical munitions. There are several possible explanations for this. First, Saddam Hussein may have differentiated between conventional and nonconventional weapons, and assumed that if the latter were to be used against Israel, it would retaliate with nonconventional ones, which in its case meant nuclear ones; and Iraq was not ready to absorb such high costs. Secondly, the United States transmitted to Saddam Hussein a clear warning that any use of chemical weapons, whether against the coalition forces, Israel or Saudi Arabia, would result in severe American punishment. Thus, for example, the US air force could have staged indiscriminate conventional bombing of Baghdad and caused its complete destruction; or US forces could have advanced on Baghdad, captured Saddam Hussein personally and put him on trial as a war criminal.

A third explanation has to do with technical questions: at that time, did Iraq have the capability to fit warheads carrying chemical munitions on its al-Hussein missiles? And, alternatively, were the Iraqis capable of transferring the chemical warheads from their arsenals to the launching sites once the war had begun? Finally, it was also thought possible at the time that a launch of warheads with chemical weapons that was scheduled to take place toward the end of the war was preempted by the activity of coalition commando units in western Iraq.

We do not have conclusive evidence to suggest which of the various explanations (or combinations thereof) deterred or prevented the use of chemical weapons. One of the arguments against the Israeli-nuclear-deterrent explanation is that Iraq did not use chemical agents anywhere--neither against the coalition forces nor against Saudi Arabia. It seems logical that this general restraint was due to a single cause, and since Israel's implied nuclear deterrent threats were clearly relevant only to attacks on Israel, they could not have constituted this cause. Failing a technical explanation, the American threats can therefore account for the general Iraqi restraint.

To sum up, the actual events of the war show that Israeli deterrent threats, some of which were interpreted as referring to nuclear retaliation for **any** Iraqi attack, failed to deter Iraq. We know that Iraq exercised restraint concerning the use of chemical weapons, but since we do not know the reasons for this restraint (and in the case of threatened use against Israel, the reasons may have been technical), we can only posit several alternative explanations.

Finally, would Israel's implied nuclear threats be effective in deterring future potential use of chemical weapons against it? The experience during the Gulf War does not provide us with strong evidence either way. It is very likely, however, that in future wars where the possibility of recourse to chemical weapons by an Arab state is raised, Israel will issue implied nuclear threats. In such circumstances, both sides would face extremely grave dilemmas.

Notes

1. Deterrence has been defined in many different ways, but the essence of the concept can be summarized as follows: **Deterrence is the threat to use military force in order to dissuade a challenger from undertaking a course of action involving the use of military force.**
   Contributions to the definition and discussion of the concept of deterrence were made by many: Bernard Brodie, Alexander George, Morton Kaplan, Thomas Milburn, George Quester, Richard Rosecrance, Bruce Russett, Thomas Schelling, Glenn Snyder. For a comprehensive contribution see Patrick M. Morgan, *Deterrence: A Conceptual Analysis* (Beverly Hills, CA: Sage Library of Social Research, 1977). The concepts of coercion and compellence are also discussed by some of the above authors.
2. Morgan, *Deterrence*.
3. It is difficult to identify a defined Israeli "strategic," let alone "deterrence" doctrine. Israeli strategic policy has remained flexible, without being fully defined or organized. For this reason I have preferred the looser term "deterrence posture."
4. For a more elaborate and detailed discussion see Yair Evron, *Israel's Nuclear Dilemma* (Ithaca: Cornell University Press, and London: Routledge, forthcoming, 1994), ch. 2. For studies of the Israeli strategic "doctrine" and deterrence see *inter alia*, Yoav Ben Horin and Barry Posen, *Israel's Strategic Doctrine* (Santa Monica: Rand, 1981); Michael Handel, *Israel's Political-Military Doctrine* (Cambridge: Center for International Affairs, Harvard University, 1973); Dan Horowitz, "Israel's Concept of Defensible Borders," (Jerusalem: Leonard Davis Institute for International Relations; Papers on Peace Problems no. 16 (Jerusalem, 1975); Dan Horowitz, "The Israeli Concept of National Security and the Prospects of Peace in the Middle East," in Gabriel Sheffer, ed., *Dynamics of a Conflict: a Re-examination of the Arab-Israeli conflict* (New York: Humanities Press, 1975); Dan Horowitz, "The Constant and the Changing in Israeli Strategic Thought" (Hebrew), in Joseph Alpher, ed., *Milchemet Breira* (Optional War) (Tel-Aviv: Hakibbutz Hameuchad Press, 1985); Dan Horowitz, "The Control of Limited Military

Operations: the Israeli Experience," in Yair Evron, ed., *International Violence: Terrorism, Surprise and Control* (Jerusalem: The Leonard Davis Institute for International Relations, 1979); Nadav Safran, *Israel, The Embattled Ally* (Cambridge, MA: Belknap Press of Harvard University Press, 1978); Ephraim Inbar, *Israeli Strategic Thought in the Post 1973 Period* (Jerusalem: Israel Research Institute of Contemporary Society, 1982); Avner Yaniv, *Deterrence Without the Bomb* (Lexington, MA: D.C. Heath, 1987). Yair Evron, *War and Intervention in Lebanon: The Israeli-Syrian Deterrence Dialogue* (London: Croom Helm, 1987).

5.   The Israeli strategy of retaliation and its effectiveness have been analyzed by several academic observers. See for example, the discussion by Horowitz, "The Israeli Experience;" Shlomo Aronson and Dan Horowitz, "The Strategy of Controlled Retaliation: The Israeli Example," *Medina Umimshal* (Hebrew), vol. 1, no. 1 (Summer 1970); Barry M. Blechman, "The Impact of Israel's Reprisals on the Behavior of the Bordering Arab Nations toward Israel," *Journal of Conflict Resolution*, vol. 16, no. 2 (June 1972). For a recent detailed and thoughtful study concentrating on the deterrence aspect of the retaliation strategy see Jonathan Shimshoni, *Israel and Conventional Deterrence* (Ithaca, NY: Cornell University Press, 1988). There are several disagreements about this strategy's objectives and functions.

6.   This concept has not as yet been suggested in the literature. Although this behavior has an element of compellence, it nevertheless serves primarily as an instrument of deterrence.

7.   The Fedayeen units which were sent on murder missions into Israel, had been organized by Egypt following and as a reaction to the Israeli raid on an Egyptian military installation near Gaza in late February 1955. Shimshoni argues that Nasser was in any case committed to a process of escalation with Israel. I disagree with his contention.

8.   Stein, in an excellent analysis, "Calculation, Miscalculation and Conventional Deterrence 1: The View From Cairo," in Robert Jervis, Janice Stein and Richard Ned Lebow, *Psychology and Deterrence* (Baltimore, MD: John Hopkins University Press, 1985), analyzes 13 cases of deterrence situations between Israel and Egypt

during 1967-1973. In some of these Israel was the challenger, in others Egypt. As the focus of this chapter is Israel's deterrence posture and its effectivity, only the more outstanding cases of successful Egyptian challenges of the status quo are considered--these took place in 1967 (failure of "specific deterrence"), in 1960/70 and in 1973. The more extensive discussion is focused only on the 1967 and 1973 wars.

9. See Haim Laskov, "Tsevet Hahafala, 1949-50," *Ma'arachot*, Nos. 191/192, 1968; and Yehuda Wallach, "Trends in the Development of Israel's Security Doctrine" (Hebrew), *Skira Hodshit*, May 1987.

10. For images of the Israeli decisionmakers during that period see Michael Brecher, *Decisions in Israel's Foreign Policy* (New Haven: Yale University Press, 1975), Chapter 6. On Ben-Gurion's assessment of the future of the military balance, see especially pp. 245-247.

11. According to a well known distinction, 'preventive war' is a war which seeks to prevent a long-term change in the balance of power; whereas 'preemptive strike' refers to the preemption of an imminent attack by the opposing side.

12. Egypt, by far the strongest Arab state, most probably viewed Israeli military superiority as very considerable. Hence the persistent Egyptian refusal to allow Syria to push it into an escalatory process with Israel. See for example Nadav Safran, *From War to War* (New York: Pegasus, 1969). For a detailed analysis of Nasser's position in this context see Benjamin Geist, *The Six-Day War: A Study in the Setting and the Process of Foreign Policy Decision Making Under Crisis Conditions* (Berkeley: University of California Press, 1980), chapter 13, specially p. 599 and fn. 31, and ch. 4. On the intensive competition in the Arab world during the first half of the '60s, see *inter alia*, Malcolm Kerr, *The Arab Cold War* (London: The Royal Institute of International Affairs, Oxford University Press, 1971).

13. The clearest statement of Egyptian deterrence intentions in the first phase of the 1967 crisis was given by Nasser in an interview published in *Look* (New York), March 19, 1968, quoted in Geist, *The Six-Day War*, ch. 13, fn. 31. Most observers, including Israelis, concur that deterrence was indeed Egypt's strategy in its initial move

into Sinai in 1967. For a contrary argument see *inter alia*, Theodor Draper, *Israel and World Politics: Roots of the Third Arab-Israeli War* (New York: Viking Press, 1968).

14. Stein, "Calculation and Miscalculation," cites several cases of Egyptian contemplation of launching an attack during the period 1967-1973, and the success of Israeli deterrence. The success was due primarily to Egyptian recognition of Israeli military superiority. One may add that this was really the reason for their caution even when Egyptian decisionmakers argued that they refrained from military operations due to the American role. For a detailed account of the process leading to the War of Attrition see Shimshoni, *Israel and Conventional Deterrence*.

15. For an extended discussion of this subject see Yair Evron, *War and Intervention in Lebanon*.

16. The War of Attrition in 1969/70 was really the first round in the 1973 War.

17. Much of the literature criticizing deterrence theory focuses on cognitive problems: misperceptions of reality (including opponent's intentions), failures in transferring accurate signals of deterrence commitments, the use of various psychological strategies to dismiss indications of adversary's resolve, etc. See for example some of the contributions in Robert Jervis, Richard Ned Lebow, *Psychology and Deterrence*; and Richard Ned Lebow and Janice Stein, "Beyond Deterrence: Building Better Theory," *Journal of Social Issues* 43 (1987).

18. Prior to the second half of the 1980s the literature on deterrence devoted little attention to different aspects of the role of the political factor in deterrence. For example, Alexander George discusses the necessity for adjusting deterrence (and coercion) to various foreign policy goals; see Alexander George, David Hall and William Simons, *The Limits of Coercive Diplomacy* (Boston: Little Brown, 1971). Bruce Russett is also concerned with the political interests under contention in deterrence situations. See his "The Calculus of Deterrence," *Journal of Conflict Resolution*, March 1963; and *idem*, "Pearl Harbor: Deterrence Theory and Decision Theory," *Journal of Peace Research*, no. 2, 1967). Richard Rosecrance points to the centrality of political constraints in "Strategic Deterrence

Reconsidered," *Adelphi Paper*, no. 116 (London: International Institute for Strategic Studies, 1975). Patrick Morgan refers to it in *Deterrence, a Conceptual Analysis*, chs. 6 and 7. See also Steven Maxwell, "Rationality in Deterrence," *Adelphi Paper*, no. 50; Robert Jervis, "Deterrence Theory Revisited," pp. 322-324, and also ch. 3 of his *Perception and Misperception in International Politics* (Boston: Little Brown, 1973). See also some of the contributions by Robert Jervis, Janice Stein and Richard Ned Lebow, in *Psychology and Deterrence*, especially Janice Stein, "Calculation; Miscalculation and Conventional Deterrence 1: The View from Cairo."

19. For more extensive treatment see Evron, *Israel's Nuclear Dilemma*. For recent discussions of the ambiguous strategy of Israel see Yair Evron, "Opaque Proliferation: The Israeli Case," *The Journal of Strategic Studies*, vol. 13, no. 3; and Avner Cohen and Marvin Miller, "Facing the Unavoidable: Israel's Nuclear Monopoly Revisited" in *idem*. The literature on Israel's nuclear posture and on the problem of proliferation in the Middle East is of course more extensive.

20. See especially in Yair Evron, *Israel's Nuclear Dilemma*, ch. 2.

21. For a detailed analysis see Evron, *Israel's Nuclear Dilemma*.

22. See the interview with Asad in *al-Qabas*, Jan. 24, 1987.

23. For further elaboration on both these uses see *ibid*.

24. This is based on Evron, *Israel's Nuclear Dilemma*, ch. 6.

25. This began with a by now famous speech by Saddam Hussein, on April 2, 1990. See the report on this speech in *The New York Times*, April 3, p. A-1.

9. Israeli Deterrence and the Gulf War[1]

Shai Feldman

On April 20, 1991, in response to the obligations stipulated in UN Resolution 687, Iraq submitted to the secretary general of the United Nations a letter detailing its nonconventional weapons arsenal and its production capacity in this realm. The letter included Iraq's first confirmation that its armed forces had possessed some 30 chemical warheads for al-Hussein surface-to-surface missiles by the end of the war.[2] During the Gulf War, some 38-42 al-Hussein missiles--armed with conventional warheads--were launched by Iraq against Israel. Baghdad's announcement accorded with the assessment made by Israeli military intelligence of Iraq's nonconventional weapons capabilities, as reflected in an interview given by its departing commander, Major General Amnon Shahak, toward the end of the war.[3] It also confirmed the evaluation of Iraq's capacities in the chemical weapons realm made by the director of research of Israeli military intelligence, Brigadier General Dani Rothchild, in a special document submitted to Israel's leaders more than three months before the war.[4]

Iraq's acknowledgement of its chemical warhead capability largely terminated a debate that began during the Gulf War: whether or not the absence of Iraqi chemical attacks against Israel during the war should be regarded as the consequence of successful Israeli deterrence. Prior to Iraq's admission, it could be argued that such attacks had not taken place simply because Iraq did not possess chemical warheads for its al-Hussein surface-to-surface missiles, and because it assessed that its SU-24 bombers--which are capable of carrying chemical ordnance--would not penetrate Israel's air defense. Indeed, many claimed that had Saddam Hussein possessed such warheads during the war--he surely would have used them. To support this claim, Iraq's conventional missile strikes against Israel during the war--as well as its refusal to withdraw from Kuwait despite the superior forces the coalition had assembled in Saudi

Arabia by the end of 1990--were taken to indicate that Saddam Hussein was not deterred, indeed, that a leader of his character could not be deterred.

The data now available--indicating that Iraq possessed chemical as well as conventional warheads during the war--requires that its wartime decision to use the latter but not the former, be explained. Accordingly, this chapter focuses on two central questions: First, to what extent can Iraq's conventional missile strikes be considered a failure of Israeli deterrence, and what were the causes of this failure? And secondly, to what extent could the fact that Iraq refrained from employing chemical warheads against Israel be considered a case of successful deterrence, and what were the causes of this success?

Addressing these questions involves a number of difficulties. Not only are the developments examined open to alternative explanations, but the effort--especially regarding the second set of questions--requires that the causes of non-events be ascertained. Thus while a particular interpretation might be regarded as persuasive, its validity will always remain subject to question.

Judgments about the wisdom of Israeli deterrence policy during the war are equally confounding, largely because it is far from clear that Israeli behavior was conditioned by a comprehensive deterrence policy. Quite the contrary, contradictions among statements made by Israeli leaders during the Gulf War indicate that a comprehensive deterrence policy was probably not debated and resolved at the time. Hence, analysis of Israeli deterrence during the war must regard the main thrust of Israeli actions and statements as merely an approximation of policy. Finally, the aforementioned contradictions in conduct must be examined, and their implications for the future assessed.

Israel's Deterrence Concept

Not every aspect of Israel's long-standing deterrence policy proved relevant in the Gulf War context. Traditionally, Israeli deterrence was designed to dissuade neighboring Arab states from invading or otherwise attacking its territory with large conventional forces. Hopefully, this was to be achieved by promising that if attacked, Israel would deliver the battle to the enemy's territory, and destroy the attacking forces there. Accordingly Yitzhak Rabin, former IDF chief of staff and later Israeli prime minister and minister of defense, often stated that "the IDF is designed to deter, and if deterrence fails--to decide the battle."

Elsewhere, this concept was elaborated by one of Israel's foremost strategists, Major General (res) Israel Tal:

> It should be remembered that our security doctrine has always asserted that the Israel Defense Forces must maintain a deterrent force, and if this fails and war breaks out, they must win it. We have never placed the capacity to deter as against the capacity to fight, but have rather regarded deterrence and the strength to win as two sides of the same coin. [Thus, Israeli] deterrence is nothing but the potential ability to win.[5]

Tal further notes that "...we have developed the doctrine of deterrence within the context of prevention and not of punishment. The concept of punishment, not as part of the concept of military decision, is foreign to our security doctrine and is, moreover, sterile."[6]

Thus, Israeli deterrence did not threaten to extract from its adversaries costs beyond those entailed in the destruction of the attacking forces. As such, it did not comprise 'deterrence by punishment,' but rather an Israeli variation of Glenn Snyder's 'deterrence by denial.'[7] In fact, its characteristics merit the designation 'deterrence by offense.' The threat that their attacking forces would be destroyed, and that some of their territory would be conquered, was expected to deter the Arab countries from assaulting the Jewish state.

To this 'general deterrence' concept, special efforts were sometimes added in order to deter specific threats. Such 'specific deterrence' was to be established by stipulating 'red lines' which, if crossed by the adversary, would lead Israel to react by force.[8] These red lines were sometimes defined in functional terms, as was the case when the freedom of navigation to Eilat was cited as a prime justification for the 1956 Sinai Campaign and the 1967 Six-Day War. On other occasions, they were defined in geographic terms: for example, when Israel communicated to Syria, in the mid-1970s, the maximum depth of Syrian military intervention in southern Lebanon that it would tolerate. Indeed, Israeli leaders sometimes referred to the possible introduction of Iraqi forces into Jordan as precisely such a casus belli.[9]

It is also noteworthy that although Israel surrounded its response to the crossing of such red lines, and to other violations of its specific deterrence threats, with much ambiguity, it was widely understood that such a response would remain within the boundaries of deterrence by offense, namely, that Israel would direct its response to the violating forces--Egyptians in the Sinai, Syrians in Lebanon, or Iraqis in Jordan--and would not engage in purposeful punishment of the perpetrators' population and/or economic infrastructure.

In practice, however, Israel was sometimes seen as reverting to countervalue punishment; this occurred in three instances, all in the context of attempting to restore specific deterrence after it had deteriorated. First, during the early 1950s, Israel often executed retaliatory punitive raids, which were at first directed against Arab villagers across its borders, in an attempt to deter them from continuing to conduct terrorism or to harbor and aid terrorists en route to Israel.[10] Later, in 1970-71, the Israel Air Force (IAF) conducted deep penetration bombings in Egypt; these were designed to damage that country's military and economic infrastructure, in order to dissuade the Egyptians from continuing to wage the War of Attrition. Finally, during the 1973 war, the IAF executed deep penetration bombings in Syria--a campaign largely directed at destroying that country's energy production capacity. Yet threats of conducting in-depth bombings were seldom incorporated into Israeli statements of its deterrence policy. Hence, none of these cases can refute the proposition that Israel largely refrained from deterrence by punishment.

Then too, as of the early 1970s, Israel's conventional deterrence, at the general and specific levels, was supplemented by the deterrent effect of Israel's perceived nuclear potential. Hence

Israel also enjoyed a measure of nonconventional deterrence by punishment. One characteristic of this deterrence is that it is supposed to affect Israel's adversaries 'through uncertainty.' That is, the Arab states' inability to rule out the possibility that Israel has acquired a nuclear arsenal is expected to deter them from confronting the Jewish state with existential threats. Accordingly, in order to avoid Israel's use of such weapons, the Arab states were to refrain from placing Israel in 'last resort' situations.[11]

The deterrent effect of Israel's nuclear potential was to be derived entirely from others' perceptions of its potency; Israel has never acknowledged possession of a nuclear arsenal. Consequently, its perceived nonconventional capabilities were never integrated into its explicit deterrence policy. Yet it is noteworthy that Israel's nuclear potential has gained much salience in recent years, and its relative role in Israel's overall deterrence package has increased accordingly. This was the consequence of a number of developments, ranging from Israel's 1981 bombing of the Osiraq reactor--which was interpreted by the Arab states as an attempt to make Israel's nuclear monopoly in the region permanent--to the infamous Vanunu affair, which was regarded by many in the Arab world as eliminating any remaining ambiguity regarding Israel's nuclear capacity.

Finally, it should be noted that the conventional and nonconventional dimensions both had a role in creating Israel's 'cumulative deterrence.' This refers to the concept developed by Israel's founding father and first prime minister, David Ben-Gurion, according to which Israel's overall, cumulative strength--and, consequently, its capacity to withstand recurring Arab threats and challenges over time--would gradually result in increased Arab awareness that Israel could not be defeated militarily. Ben-Gurion hoped that, in turn, this would lead the Arabs to conclude that there was little point in maintaining the state of conflict and war with the Jewish state, and that it would be far preferable to reach an accommodation, to the benefit of all states in the region. Thus, Israel's first prime minister believed that a peaceful settlement of the Arab-Israeli dispute would not evolve until Israel's cumulative deterrence was established.

Israeli Deterrence in the Gulf War

As indicated earlier, not all components of Israel's traditional concept of conventional deterrence were relevant to the threats presented by Iraq during the Gulf crisis and the subsequent war. At the outset, it became clear that Israel was likely to face three distinct Iraqi threats. In the conventional realm: the possible introduction into Jordan of limited Iraqi forces, up to a number of divisions of relatively low quality; and/or, a conventional missile strike against Israel's population centers.[12] And, in the nonconventional realm, a possible Iraqi chemical weapons attack on the Jewish state.[13]

The first two threats resulted from Saddam's anticipated effort to break up the Arab coalition supporting the US, by transforming the crisis into an expression of the Arab-Israel conflict. Clearly Iraq could only hope to achieve this if it managed to entice Israel into intervening militarily in the conflict. In turn, such an intervention could only be gained by presenting Israel with a threat to which it felt compelled to respond forcefully. Iraq was likely to try to obtain this objective by introducing units of its armed forces into Jordan and/or by striking Israel's population centers with surface-to-surface missiles. In other words, the Iraqis were expected to reason that in light of Israel's 'red lines' with respect to the threat to its security embodied in the introduction of foreign forces into Jordan, and in view of Israel's inherent sensitivity to civilian casualties from missile attacks, it would regard such moves as intolerable, and would respond by intervening forcefully.

The third threat that Israel was expected to confront--possible Iraqi use of chemical weapons against it, delivered either by air power or by surface-to-surface missiles--could have occurred in an attempt to obtain Israel's intervention through escalation, following a prior failure to achieve this by lesser means. Alternatively, such an attack could have been conducted in the context of a much wider Iraqi quest for leadership of the Arab world. That is, by attacking Israel with surface-to-surface missiles with chemical warheads, Iraq could have attempted to support its claim to be the only Arab state capable of matching Israel's edge in the realm of nonconventional weapons. Such a move could have been incorporated into Iraq's general effort to delegitimize Arab governments that took part in the coalition confronting Iraq in the Gulf Crisis.

Further, an Iraqi chemical strike against Israel could have been conducted as an act of despair; namely, in the context of a 'last resort' effort to avert a massive defeat that threatened Saddam Hussein's regime.[14] Thus the Iraqis could have hoped that if Israel were to suffer heavy casualties and to sustain much damage, it would pressure Washington to cease its fire so that additional costs would be averted.

Clearly, the threat implied by Israel's traditional concept of deterrence by offense did not deter Saddam Hussein from launching his conventionally armed surface-to-surface missiles against Israel during the Gulf War. But this merely points to the limitations of Israel's deterrence concept: it has limited application beyond the efforts to dissuade an attack by the large conventional forces of Arab states that are contiguous to Israel. The application of deterrence by offense to the case of the Gulf War--an implied Israeli threat to destroy the Iraqi surface-to-surface missile launchers--could not deter Saddam Hussein: as indicated earlier, Saddam's decision to strike Israel was informed not by the failure of Israel's implied threat to respond, but rather as a consequence of its credibility. Direct Israeli intervention held Saddam's only hope of breaking the coalition confronting him by transforming the nature of the crisis, and would thereby have served his interests. Thus Iraq's leader attacked Israel not despite, but rather because he thought he could count on Israel to respond.

Indeed, in terms of deterrence, Saddam's decisions to invade Kuwait and to attack Israel were propelled by very different causes. In the first instance, at root was a gross underestimation of Washington's resolve and consequent odds of response. In this sense, Iraq's leader proved to be a victim of the Vietnam syndrome: clearly, he was convinced that the US lacked sufficient determination, and would therefore refrain from reacting to Kuwait's conquest, as well as to the subsequent redeployment of Iraqi forces along the Kuwaiti-Saudi border.

Saddam Hussein's estimate of America's likely response was probably also informed by Washington's conduct vis-a-vis Iraq during the year preceding the invasion. Most likely, he viewed a series of statements made by senior administration officials--including the now-famous discussion he held with US Ambassador April Glaspie on July 25, 1990--as indicating that the Bush administration might tolerate an invasion of Kuwait.[15] More important, he probably read the active lobbying conducted by the administration on Capitol Hill in 1989-90--which was designed to avert a congressional imposition of sanctions against Iraq--as indicating that President Bush was not interested in a direct confrontation with Baghdad.[16]

In contrast, Saddam's calculus with respect to Israel was quite the opposite. Here deterrence failed not because Saddam underestimated Israel's capabilities and determination, but rather because he assessed Israel's resolve as high, and was therefore confident that his attack would produce its desired intervention. Paradoxically, therefore, Israel's failure to dissuade Iraq should be primarily attributed to the success of its deterrent.

In turn, Israel was propelled by four considerations to refrain from responding to Iraq's surface-to-surface missile attacks: The first and most important was Israel's own estimate--which paralleled Washington's and Baghdad's--that its intervention would complicate the task of maintaining the Arab states' participation in the anti-Iraq coalition. Given the magnitude of Iraq's threat to the Jewish state, Israel had a clear grand-strategic interest in seeing Iraq's power cut down to size, hence, in refraining from doing anything that might undermine this task. As such, Israel had good reasons of its own to avoid damaging the unity of the coalition confronting Iraq. IDF Chief of Staff Dan Shomron expressed this view during the war:

> Israel has several objectives. I regard the destruction of the Eastern Front--which is taking place by the day and by the hour--as our objective.... The decision not to react at this stage is the consequence not only of political considerations, but [also] of political-military considerations--a consideration of our national security.... We must make a comprehensive assessment: would it really serve our purpose to provide Saddam Hussein with an excuse to withdraw from Kuwait, to stop the war when he is still in power and when part of

his army remains intact, arguing that the real problem of the Arab nation, whose representative he considers himself to be, is Israel?[17]

The second grand-strategic consideration informing Israel's restraint was that by demonstrating its sensitivity to America's priorities and concerns--and in view of the Bush administration's explicit pleas that Israel restrain its reaction to Iraq's missile attacks--its strategic alliance with the US could be strengthened and long-term benefits could be derived. To the extent that these benefits would add to Israel's overall power, they could be regarded as a contribution to the Jewish state's cumulative deterrent.

The Israeli government was further led to understand that some immediate benefits could also be derived if it avoided a response to Iraq's missile attacks. These included an increase in direct and indirect US military and economic aid--in the form of special economic assistance, which was later determined at a level of $650 million;[18] approval for Israel to "draw-down" from US military surpluses in Europe at a level of $700 million, as well as final consent to a US government guarantee for a $400 million loan for new immigrant housing;[19] and the stationing of Patriot anti-aircraft and anti-missile missile batteries in Israel. Indeed, the latter act comprised a new milestone in US-Israeli strategic cooperation and in America's commitment to Israel: for the first time in Israel's history, American combat units were sent to take an active part in its defense. This comprised a clear signal of America's commitment to Israel's security, and thus a significant contribution to Israel's cumulative deterrence.

Thus, Israel's decision to refrain from a military response to Iraq's missile attacks improved the odds of obtaining two objectives that significantly affected its overall strategic standing: maintaining an environment in which the coalition forces could continue diminishing Iraq's power, and strengthening the alliance with the United States. And, although Israel's restraint might have eroded somewhat the credibility of its immediate deterrence--since some damage to Israel's reputation, as a state which never permits such attacks to pass without a response, could not be avoided--this potential source of erosion was more than compensated by the payoffs Israel received as a consequence of its restraint. In turn, these payoffs comprised a significant contribution to Israel's cumulative deterrence.

The third consideration leading to Israel's restraint concerned the limited availability of options for cost-effective response. Primarily, its options for retaliating against Iraq were limited by the fact that prior approval of the allies was needed if Israeli air assets were to be introduced into an area that comprised part of the coalition's theater of operations. This approval was not forthcoming, as it would have connoted tacit acceptance by the Arab members of the coalition--primarily Saudi Arabia, but also Syria--of Israel's participation in the hostilities.

Conversely, Israel could not attempt a surprise attack against Iraq's missile launchers since--contrary to the situation prevailing when it conducted its strike against Iraq's Osiraq nuclear reactor in 1981--the air defense systems of Iraq, Syria, Jordan, and Saudi Arabia were now at their highest state of alert. Further, the imperative of avoiding an accidental confrontation with US forces-- which could have led to tragic consequences, similar to those associated with Israel's accidental 1967 attack on the USS Liberty-- induced much reluctance to attempt such a surprise. Without proper coordination with US forces, whereby the Israel Air Force would have received the means for discriminating coalition aircraft from Iraqi aircraft (IFF--Identification Friend or Foe--systems), as well as the means for allowing coalition aircraft to identify the Israeli aircraft as "friends," such an attack could not be executed without intolerable operational and political risks. These considerations guided Israeli decisionmakers, and they made this clear publicly during the war.[20]

In addition, it is far from clear that Israel was assured of its capacity to conduct an effective counteroffensive attack against Iraq's surface-to-surface missile launchers. Indeed, while there is little doubt regarding the IAF's experience in destroying such targets when their location is ascertained with great precision, it is not certain that this condition could be met with respect to Iraq's mobile launchers. Thus, target acquisition in this case might have proved to be an extremely demanding enterprise. An Israeli operation that was less than entirely successful in light of these constraints, would have eroded Israel's reputation, thus damaging the cumulative deterrence that it has successfully acquired over the years.

In turn, it was widely reported internationally that problems in locating Iraq's missile launchers might have propelled Israel to attempt a 'vertical indirect approach' by landing airborne or heliborne forces for a search-and-destroy mission in western Iraq.[21] But such an effort would have been even more confounding: in the first place, coordination with the allies--which was completely out of the question in the case of an Israeli 'invasion' of Iraq--was even more critical if ground forces were to be transported and landed. Without such coordination, Israeli ground forces might have been bombed by the allies' aircraft operating in the area. More important, Israel's political leadership was extremely unlikely to approve the dropping of large forces that could not be easily extracted from the theater of operations, were they to encounter unexpected resistance. This was particularly demanding given the fact that the airspace of hostile countries would have had to be violated were Israel to mount support operations or rescue missions.

Thus, it seems that Israel could not establish effective deterrence by denial vis-a-vis the threat of Iraqi missile attacks during the Gulf War; its options for denying Saddam Hussein's capacity to launch surface-to-surface missiles from western Iraq were, at best, very risky. And, paradoxically, Saddam was unlikely to be deterred even had Israel possessed readily available denial options, since its military intervention would merely have served his purpose.

Yet the odds of establishing effective deterrence by punishment against Iraq's conventional missile attacks were even lower. A punitive strike directed at Iraq's 'values' would have required that the IAF penetrate Iraq in depth. This would have made prior coordination with the allies even more critical, since Israel's aircraft would have had to operate in an area that comprised the main theater of operations for over 2,000 coalition sorties daily. More important, given the intensity of the allies' air campaign against Iraq's infrastructure--and the resulting magnitude of the punishment already experienced by Iraq--and in view of the IAF's limited capacity for bombing at great distances, an Israeli air strike probably would not have registered a significant mark on Baghdad's leaders. This point was raised by the former commander of the Israel Air Force, Major General (res) Benjamin (Benny) Peled, in an interview during the war: "What can we do more than the Americans' massive bombing?" he asked rhetorically.[22] Thus, the marginal effects of an Israeli punitive strike were unlikely to deter Iraq from conducting further surface-to-surface missile attacks.

Finally, Israel's restraint was also made easier by the fact that the damage caused by Iraq's missile attacks during the war remained limited. Although considerable structural damage was incurred, the number of casualties caused by these attacks was minuscule. Had Israel suffered much higher casualties as a consequence of the Iraqi attacks, its government would have faced far greater internal pressures to respond. Instead, a majority of Israelis supported their government's policy of restraint. In three separate public opinion polls conducted during the war--between mid-January and early February--over 80 percent of the respondents opted for Israel to continue refraining from a military response to Iraq's al-Hussein missile attacks.[23]

Thus the limited damage incurred by Israel as a consequence of Iraq's missile attacks further complicated the task of deterrence. Simply, it was not easy to create Iraqi fear that Israel might retaliate disproportionately while the Israeli public continued to favor restraint. As long as the effects of the Iraqi strikes remained limited, the Israeli government could obtain neither the minimal international legitimacy nor the required domestic support for threatening credibly to invoke the threat of disproportional retaliation, e.g. by issuing a nuclear threat. The political and other costs that Israel would have incurred had it attempted to utilize such a threat--against the limited challenge of Iraq's missile attacks--would have been prohibitive.

Thus, not only was the 'balance of capabilities' in Iraq's favor--the latter could easily launch its missiles against Israel's population centers, while Israel's options for effective 'denial' or punitive responses were both limited and confounding--but the 'balance of resolve' seems to have favored Baghdad as well. Saddam Hussein had a strong interest in obtaining Israel's intervention, while the Israeli government understood that its response would merely serve Iraq's objectives, and that it could not easily present itself as being compelled to respond disproportionately. Hence, Iraq enjoyed an advantage in both central components of deterrence: capabilities and resolve. Under such conditions, Israel was extremely unlikely to deter Saddam from attacking its cities with conventionally armed surface-to-surface missiles.

Yet, had Israel fully understood in advance that attempts to **deter** such strikes were bound to fail--precisely because Saddam Hussein's objectives would have been served by a forceful Israeli response--its goal of **dissuading** Iraq from striking its population centers would have been better met by **not** committing itself so forcefully to respond to such attacks. In fact, such an alternative declaratory policy, emphasizing that Israel's response should not be reflexive or automatic, was suggested, at least at one point, by IDF Chief of Staff Dan Shomron, who stated on September 16, 1990:

> This is not an automatic situation, in which one Iraqi soldier steps on an electronic fence and everything starts flying. We are now in the midst of an international crisis, in which the United States is involved, and every situation requires careful consideration. The entry of Iraqi troops into Jordan will not automatically trigger an Israeli military move. We will first examine what Iraqi troops are sent to Jordan and why, and how IDF intervention would affect the western Arab coalition in the Persian Gulf.[24]

A similar approach was suggested in December by Yitzhak Rabin, then solely a member of Parliament: "We should not respond automatically to an Iraqi missile strike against Israel. Rather, we should consider our steps carefully, so that we do not fall into the trap which Saddam Hussein is preparing for us."[25] Later, Major General (res) Aharon Yariv, head of Tel Aviv University's Jaffee Center for Strategic Studies, at a press conference on January 6, 1991 also suggested that Israel follow precisely such a more flexible approach: "Even if Iraq strikes Israel, through the use of missiles or airpower, we should consider the possibility of refraining from a response, so that we do not get entangled in the war."[26] Yariv added that "if the damage caused by the Iraqi attack is limited, Israel would have to weigh carefully whether to respond. An Israeli response would play into the hands of Saddam Hussein, who will be interested in transforming the war in the Gulf into an Arab-Israeli war."[27] Yariv's suggestion was supported the following morning, in an editorial, by Israel's leading morning newspaper, *Ha'aretz*.[28]

Unfortunately, most of Israel's political leadership continued to warn, throughout the crisis and until war broke out, that Israel's response to the introduction of Iraqi troops into Jordan, and to any Iraqi attack on Israel, would be immediate and forceful: "Israel would regard any Iraqi effort to advance forces into Jordan as a provocative step that could provoke a military strike. We will not permit the entry of Iraqi troops into Jordan. This has been a long standing Israeli policy."[29] Thus, Prime Minister Yitzhak Shamir, speaking at the National Security College on August 9, 1990, said that "anyone attempting an attack on Israel will be bringing upon himself a great disaster."[30] Less than a week later, Defense Minister Moshe Arens warned Saddam Hussein that he would encounter "a forceful Israeli response from the air" if he attacked Israel. Regarding the possibility of the entry of Iraqi forces into Jordan, Arens said: "we will react immediately with force, and I think this is well known in Baghdad."[31]

Interestingly, Prime Minister Shamir apparently was not aware of the internal contradictions in the statements he made to Israel Television on August 22. In his interview on the program 'Moked,' Shamir argued that "Israel has no interest in helping Saddam Hussein to get us embroiled in the Gulf crisis." On the other hand, he claimed that "the parties contemplating an attack on Israel know very well they will pay a terrible price should they attempt such an attack."[32] There is no evidence that Shamir was cognizant of the fact that the very promise to respond to any Iraqi aggression might encourage Saddam to attack Israel in order to embroil it in the Gulf Crisis. Similarly, Chief of Staff Shomron, on August 25, admitted on the one hand that "Saddam has an interest in bringing Israel into the picture as the Arab states' common enemy," and on the other argued that "in light of [Israel's] deterrent capacity, it is not likely that Saddam Hussein will attempt to open a second front by attacking Israel."[33]

On August 30, in response to Iraqi threats, Prime Minister Shamir repeated his warning: "In the past, Israel has demonstrated its capacity to defend itself. If we are attacked by Iraq, we will repel the attack and the attacker will regret his action."[34] The prime minister, as well as Deputy Foreign Minister Benyamin Netanyahu, issued similar warnings on September 24.[35] These statements were amplified by Foreign Minister David Levy, who on September 26 warned that "whoever attacks Israel won't live to remember it."[36] In a speech to the UN General Assembly on October 1, Levy again warned that "Israel will know how to defend itself if attacked, and its punch will be hard and painful."[37] Prime Minister Shamir added a few days later that "if Saddam Hussein attacks Israel, he will be making a terrible mistake and will pay for it dearly."[38]

In November, Defense Minister Arens repeated Israel's threat: "Any Iraqi attempt to involve Israel would comprise a grave error on its part. If Israel were attacked, it would respond in a fashion that would not be 'low profile.'"[39] In late December, Prime Minister Shamir stated again: "we repeat that if the threats materialize, we will strike back in a most forceful manner." At the same time Arens said: "Saddam Hussein knows that if attacked, Israel will respond, and will respond with great force."[40]

Only a week before the war, on January 9, 1991, Foreign Minister Levy repeated these warnings in a conversation with 25 visiting US congressmen: "If attacked, Israel will retaliate to defend its security and the security of its citizens."[41] The following day, Defense Minister Arens argued that "Iraq's capacity to harm Israel is very limited, but if we are attacked, we will respond without hesitation."[42] Two days later, Chief of Staff Shomron repeated his warning to the effect that Saddam Hussein had better take into account "a very forceful response by Israel in case of an Iraqi attack or an attempted Iraqi attack." Defense Minister Arens, in a visit to an air base in the country's north, promised that "if Israel is attacked, it would utilize its legitimate right to respond."[43]

Had Yariv's suggestion been accepted, the exception to Israeli deterrence policy could have been explained in terms of the unique circumstances prevailing, which allowed Israel to obtain its aforementioned grand-strategic objectives by restraining its conduct. Thus, doubts might have been created in Saddam Hussein's mind regarding his chances of obtaining Israel's intervention by attacking its cities. Conceivably, such a declaratory policy might have diminished his incentives to launch such strikes. More important, it would have limited whatever potential damage Israeli deterrence might suffer as a consequence of its recent exercise in restraint.

In the event, Israel refrained from adopting a flexible declaratory policy, and thereby nurtured Saddam Hussein's hope that he might obtain Israel's intervention by striking at its population centers. Even after the war had already begun, and despite the important considerations that led to Israel's decision to restrain its response to Iraq's surface-to-surface missile attacks, its spokespersons continued to provide Saddam reason to believe that should he sustain his attacks long enough, he might still provoke Israel's involvement. Thus, General Shomron stated a few days after the al-Hussein missile attacks began that the United States was aware that "we are not willing to absorb additional attacks without responding [to them]."[44]

Withal, it is important to avoid exaggerating the possible negative impact of Israel's conduct during the Gulf War on the credibility of its deterrence. Far more important than Israel's failure to deter the limited challenge presented by Iraq's conventional missiles, was its apparent success in deterring Iraqi use of chemical weapons. Without this achievement, Israel might have suffered Iraqi chemical attacks, delivered either by bombers--primarily the Soviet-made Su-24s--or by surface-to-surface missiles, notably the 600-km range al-Husseins. That Israel dissuaded Iraq from exercising either option was largely due to its novel application of deterrence by punishment, but complemented by some measure of deterrence by denial.

Deterrence by denial against Iraqi chemical attacks was exercised by implementing a combination of passive and active defense. On the passive side, as the crisis unfolded, Israel decided to implement a basket of civil defense measures. Primarily, this entailed equipping the entire population with gas masks, and issuing instructions for reducing vulnerability to chemical toxins, e.g., by sealing a room in each house and apartment against such attacks.⁴⁵ This was done despite initial opposition, within the IDF and the Defense Ministry, to the distribution of chemical protective equipment, on the grounds that such measures could not be justified by Iraq's limited capabilities in this realm.⁴⁶

As for active defense, the Israel Air Force was placed on the highest alert status and intensified its air patrols dramatically, to be ready to intercept incoming Iraqi aircraft carrying chemical ordnance.⁴⁷ Israel gave a clearly deterrent dimension to its activity in this realm when the commander of its Air Force, Major General Avihu Bin-Nun, announced that the force under his command was on the highest state of alert in anticipation of a possible confrontation with Iraq, and that "pilots are sitting in their aircraft ready for any contingency."⁴⁸

In addition, at Jerusalem's request, the United States stationed Patriot anti-aircraft and anti-missile missile batteries to protect Israel's population centers. By the end of the war, eight batteries of Patriot missiles had been stationed in Israel: two had been purchased from the United States by the IDF before the war; four were US Army units brought to Israel shortly after the war began; one was donated by West Germany and operated by a joint US-Israeli team; and one was a Dutch unit that the Hague offered to station in Israel during the war.⁴⁹ The Patriot deployment may also have been designed to affect Saddam's calculations with respect to his capacity to penetrate Israel's airspace.

While these denial measures may have played some role in affecting Iraq's calculation, it is much more likely that Saddam Hussein's conduct was conditioned by Israel's effective deterrence by punishment. Thus, his decision to refrain from attacking Israel with chemical weapons was largely propelled by his fear of possible Israeli nuclear retaliation. Whether by accident or design, Israeli statements before and during the Gulf War--and, in at least one instance, American statements as well--must have enhanced Saddam's fear that he might well suffer nuclear punishment in response to an Iraqi chemical attack on the Jewish state.

In view of the proliferation of missiles and chemical weapons in the region in recent years, Israeli leaders were often asked to define Israel's response to the threat of attack by such weapons. The issue was at times sharpened by a vocal Arab threat to employ such weapons. This was the case when Saddam Hussein, in a speech he delivered on April 2, 1990, threatened that if Iraq were attacked he would make use of 'binary' weapons that would "consume half of Israel."[50] Israeli leaders responded with counterthreats that comprised a combination of deterrence by denial and deterrence by punishment. While Prime Minister Shamir would only say that "Israel knows how to defend itself," Defense Minister Rabin acknowledged that "we have the means for a devastating response, many times greater than [the magnitude of] Saddam Hussein's threats."[51]

Indeed, in mid-February 1991 Rabin (now once again only a member of Knesset) seemed to confirm that with regard to the Arabs' missile threat, Israeli policy relied exclusively on the deterrent effect of its capacity to punish by wiping out Arab population centers. In a speech to the Labor Party's members of Knesset, he reportedly said: "How do you think we deterred the Syrians? What did we tell them? We told them: 'if you strike Tel Aviv with surface-to-surface missiles--Damascus will be destroyed. If you attack Haifa with such missiles, Damascus and Haleb will not remain--they would be destroyed. We will not deal with the missile launchers, we will destroy Damascus instead."[52]

These expressions of Israel's deterrence by punishment policy vis-a-vis the threat of an Arab missile and chemical attack, were embellished following the outbreak of the Gulf War by a number of statements that seemed to deviate from longstanding Israeli declaratory policy regarding the state's nuclear potential. Until this time, Israeli leaders had maintained consistently that "Israel would not be the first to introduce nuclear weapons into the Middle East." Sometimes, Israeli leaders added that "neither would Israel be the second"--meaning that it would introduce such weapons the moment they were introduced by an Arab state, and implying that Israel already possessed the potential for such an immediate response.[53]

Yet on December 29, 1990 in a speech to the Commerce and Industry Club in Tel Aviv, the IDF's Shomron stated that "Israel would not be the first **to use** nuclear weapons in the Middle East."[54]

As far as could be ascertained, General Shomron simply mis-spoke on that occasion, and his deviation from standing policy was completely unintentional. Unaware of this, however, Israel's ambassador to the United States, Zalman Shoval, took Shomron's words as a signal that Israel's declaratory policy regarding its nuclear potential had changed, and he repeated the chief of staff's statement.[55] Three weeks later, the statement was repeated again, this time by Israel's ambassador to Belgium.[56]

It would be hardly surprising if the cumulative effect of the statements were regarded in the Arab world as a purposeful move by Israel to take its nuclear potential "out of the basement."[57] While Shomron's statement could have weakened Israeli deterrence by punishment of an Iraqi chemical strike by indicating that it would not embark upon nuclear retaliation following a non-nuclear attack, it was more widely regarded as enhancing deterrence by seeming to suggest that Israel had already introduced nuclear weapons to the region.

The final contribution to the enhancement of Israeli nuclear deterrence of an Iraqi chemical attack came from an unexpected source: American Secretary of Defense Richard Cheney. In an interview to CNN on February 2, the secretary was asked why, in his opinion, Saddam Hussein had so far refrained from attacking Israel with chemical weapons. Cheney responded: "I assume that he knows that if he were to resort to chemical weapons--that that would be an escalation to weapons of mass destruction and that the possibility would then exist--certainly with respect to the Israelis, for example--that they might retaliate with unconventional weapons as well. And I think that the uncertainty that is there might have discouraged him." Cheney preferred not to go into details regarding Israel's nonconventional arsenal. But when, later in the interview, he was asked whether in his view Israel would respond with tactical nuclear weapons to an Iraqi chemical attack, Cheney responded: "That decision the Israelis would have to make--but I would think that he [Saddam] has to be cautious in terms of how he proceeds in his attacks against Israel."[58] The US Secretary of Defense thus refrained from any comment regarding the premise that informed the question--namely, an implied Israeli nonconventional nuclear arsenal which it could utilize in the framework of such retaliation. Even more important was the fact that Cheney avoided any expression of disapproval regarding such possible retaliation. Consequently, the American secretary of defense's reply could be interpreted as confirming legitimacy upon Israel's nuclear potential and, hence, as a significant contribution to its deterrent capacity.

The next day, Defense Minister Arens acknowledged Secretary Cheney's statement, while still attempting to preserve a measure of ambiguity surrounding Israel's nuclear potential: "I think he [Cheney] said that Saddam has reasons to worry--yes, he does have reasons to worry." In response to a query whether this includes fear of nuclear retaliation, Arens said: "Cheney did not talk specifically, and I would not have expected him to do so under present circumstances. But if you say that Saddam has reasons to worry--this is correct."[59]

These deterrence boosters were somewhat balanced during the war by two developments that threatened to erode the credibility of Israeli deterrence--though in retrospect they seem to have had an extremely marginal effect on Israel's environment. In the first instance, there was a possibility that Israel's decision to adopt passive defense measures--sealing rooms, the distribution of gas masks--might be interpreted by Saddam Hussein as implying Israeli willingness to sustain chemical attacks. This concern was fueled by the fact that Israel did not accompany these measures with an associated declaratory policy clarifying that these means were adopted merely to diminish the consequences of the first chemical attack, and that Israel would retaliate and inflict heavy punishment before a second attack were ever mounted.

Yet this omission evidently had no material effect on the Arabs' perception of Israeli determination. The steps taken by Israel were probably interpreted as implying that it merely sought to complement its nuclear deterrence by punishment with a limited measure of deterrence by denial. Hence, Israel's decision to implement strict civil defense measures probably did not affect its overall deterrent.

A second, and temporarily more worrisome development, concerned a statement made by Defense Minister Arens. In a

Cabinet meeting on January 27, Arens noted that by attacking Israel's cities with conventionally armed surface-to-surface missiles, the Iraqis had already crossed Israel's 'red lines,' and that, therefore, "the IDF's response can be expected, with its dimensions and objectives to be determined [in the future]."[60] The defense minister's statement, which was immediately leaked to the press, could have been interpreted as implying that no additional red lines remained following Iraq's conventional attacks, and that Israel did not regard a chemical attack on its population centers as comprising a significantly greater threat which, in turn, would unleash a very different Israeli response.

Realizing the potential damage that Arens' statement could cause to Israeli deterrence of possible Iraqi chemical attacks, a number of Israeli leaders, including IDF Deputy Chief of Staff Ehud Barak, soon moved to correct the defense minister's error. In an interview he granted to military correspondents on February 3, Barak was asked to define what comprised Israel's red line: what aggressive act, if carried out, would lead Israel to launch a counter-operation. Barak responded: "Iraqi use of nonconventional weapons against Israel."[61] As noted earlier, Defense Minister Arens himself moved to limit any damage his earlier statement could have made by granting support to the declaration made by US Secretary of Defense Cheney with respect to Israel's likely response in the event of an Iraqi chemical attack.

In any case, these possible sources of damage to Israel's wartime deterrence against possible Iraqi chemical attacks were far less significant than the aforementioned three contributions to the salience of Israeli nuclear deterrence which evolved during the war. In turn, these contributions merely added to Iraq's longstanding assessment that Israel possessed a nuclear arsenal and might employ it under some circumstances.[62]

Indeed, contrary to its calculus with respect to the employment of conventionally armed missiles, in pondering a possible chemical attack Iraq probably judged that Israel possessed both the capability and the resolve to activate its nuclear deterrent. Saddam is likely to have judged that the Israeli government would enjoy sufficient domestic support if it invoked its nuclear deterrent in response to an Iraqi chemical attack, and that if Israel were to do so under extreme circumstances--it might even enjoy considerable international legitimacy, as reflected in Secretary Cheney's responses. Not surprisingly, therefore, Israel's enhanced nuclear deterrence appears to have successfully dissuaded Iraq from attacking its cities with chemical weapons during the Gulf War.

Notes

1. This chapter was originally published in *War in the Gulf: Implications for Israel*, Report of a JCSS Study Group, ed. Joseph Alpher (Jerusalem: Jerusalem Post, 1992).
2. Ori Nir, "US Rejects Iraqi Report on its Nonconventional Arsenal," *Ha'aretz*, April 24, 1990.
3. Eitan Rabin, "Head of MI, General Shahak: Iraq has Chemical Capability," *Ha'aretz*, February 15, 1991; Dani Sade, "Head of MI: Iraq has Chemical Missiles," *Yediot Aharonot*, February 15, 1991.
4. Amira Segev, "Looking for Rothchild," *Hadashot*, March 1, 1991.
5. Israel Tal, "Israel's Security in the Eighties," *Jerusalem Quarterly*, no. 17 (Fall 1980), pp. 13-18.
6. *Ibid.*, p. 14.
7. See Glenn Snyder, "Deterrence by Denial and Punishment," in David Bobrow, ed., *Components of Defense Policy*, pp. 209-237 (Chicago: Rand McNally, 1965).
8. See Micha Bar, *Red Lines in Israel's Deterrence Strategy* (Tel Aviv: Ma'arachot, 1990).
9. *Ibid.*, pp. 97-99.
10. See Jonathan Shimshoni, *Israel and Conventional Deterrence* (Ithaca: Cornell University Press, 1988). As Shimshoni points out, Israel's retaliatory raids were later redirected from civilian villages to Jordanian and Egyptian police and military installations.
11. See Shai Feldman, *Israeli Nuclear Deterrence* (New York: Columbia University Press, 1982).
12. Akiva Eldar *et al.*, "Evaluation in Jerusalem: Iraq may Initiate Missile Attack Against Israel," *Ha'aretz*, August 9, 1990.
13. "Minister Arens: I Am Relaxed; no Need to Distribute Gas Masks Now," *Ma'ariv*, August 10, 1990.
14. Amos Gilboa, "Saddam's Interest in Employing Chemical Weapons Increases," *Ma'ariv*, January 29, 1991; Zadok Yeheskeli, "What Took Place Until Now is Kids' Play," *Yediot Aharonot*, February 21, 1991.

15. See Jim Hoagland, "Transcript Shows Muted US Response to Threat by Saddam in Late July," *Washington Post*, September 13, 1990.
16. See "Bush Accused of Sending Confusing Signals to Iraq Before Invasion," *Chicago Tribune*, March 22, 1991.
17. Amir Oren et al., "IDF Operation Against Scuds May Allow Hussein's Survival," *Davar*, February 2, 1991.
18. Thomas L. Friedman, "US Agrees to Give Israel $650 Million for War Expenses," *International Herald Tribune (IHT)*, March 7, 1991.
19. Joel Brinkley, "US Loan Too Little for Israel," *IHT*, February 22, 1991.
20. Ronald J Ostrow and Robin Wright, "To Strike, Israel Needs 'Friend' I.D.," *IHT*, January 28, 1991; see also Akiva Eldar and Ori Nir, "Political Source: Israel will Attack only in Coordination with the US; Will Respond only if more Missiles Land," *Ha'aretz*, January 21, 1991; Ori Nir, "Arens: US Rejection of Military Coordination Prevents IDF Response," *Ha'aretz*, January 28, 1991.
21. See Avi Raz, "The Commando will Attack the Missiles," *Ma'ariv*, February 2, 1991; Ori Nir, "Israel Wanted to Land Forces in Iraq in Order to Destroy Missile Launchers," *Ha'aretz*, March 8, 1991.
22. "Iraq May Send Bombers to Israel, Loaded with Chemical Bombs," *Hadashot*, February 8, 1991.
23. "Most Support Restraint Regarding Missile Firings," *Ma'ariv*, February 8, 1991; Dani Kipper, "Majority of Public Supports Restraint," *Yediot Aharonot*, February 21, 1991.
24. Joshua Brilliant, "No Automatic Response if Iraqi Troops Enter Jordan," *Jerusalem Post*, September 17, 1990; see also "CoS: 'We will not Respond Automatically to the Entry of Iraqis into Jordan,'" *Ma'ariv*, September 17, 1990.
25. "Levy: 'Israel Must Respond with Determination in case of Iraqi Aggression,'" *Ma'ariv*, December 30, 1990.
26. Eitan Rabin, "Aharon Yariv: 'Israel Must Consider the Need to Avoid Getting Embroiled [in the war] Even if Saddam Attacks,'" *Ha'aretz*, January 7, 1991.
27. "Well Calculated Response," *Ha'aretz*, January 8, 1991.

28. *Ha'aretz*, January 8, 1991.
29. See Jackson Diehl, "Israel, Urging Stiff Sanctions, Tells Iraq to Stay Out of Jordan," *IHT*, August 8, 1990. See also Yosef Zuriel, "Israel will Act if Iraq Enters Jordan," *Ma'ariv*, August 8, 1990; Ze'ev Schiff, "Israel Presents a Determined Red Line," *Ha'aretz*, August 8, 1990.
30. On Levy and Chami Shalev, "Arens: 'I am Calm;' Security Sources: 'Saddam Does not have Chemical Warheads,'" *Davar*, August 10, 1990.
31. Yosef Zuriel, "Arens: 'We Will React Forcefully if Iraq Enters Jordan,'" *Ma'ariv*, August 16, 1990; Joshua Brilliant, "Arens Again Warns Iraq Against Strike," *Jerusalem Post*, August 16, 1990.
32. "Shamir on 'Moked': 'If They Dare Attack Us, They Will Pay a Terrible Price,'" *Ha'aretz*, August 23, 1990.
33. "The CoS: 'Israel is not in a State of Emergency,'" *Ma'ariv*, August 26, 1990; Joshua Brilliant, "Arens and Shomron Say Attack Not Likely Because of Israel's Strength," *Jerusalem Post*, August 26, 1990.
34. Eitan Rabin, "Shamir: 'Whoever Attacks Us will Regret It,'" *Ma'ariv*, August 31, 1990.
35. Avinoam Bar Yosef, "Netanyahu: 'Iraqi Damage to Israel will Endanger Arab States' Interests,'" *Ma'ariv*, September 25, 1990; Baruch Me'iri, "Shamir: 'If Iraq Attacks--We will Strike Her,'" *Ma'ariv*, September 25, 1991; Dan Izenberg, "Shamir: 'We are Preparing Ourselves,'" *Jerusalem Post*, September 26, 1990.
36. David Makovsky, "Levy: 'Those who Attack Israel Won't Live to Remember,'" *Jerusalem Post*, September 27, 1990.
37. Shlomo Shamir, "Levy at UN: 'If Israel is Attacked by Iraq--It Will Operate Immediately and Independently,'" *Ha'aretz*, October 2, 1990.
38. Shefi Gabai *et al.*, "Iraq: 'War Preferable to Surrender,'" *Ma'ariv*, October 5, 1990.
39. Eitan Rabin *et al.*, "Arens: 'If Israel is Attacked by Iraq, its Response would not be "Low Profile,"'" *Ha'aretz*, November 7, 1990.
40. "IDF on Top Alert; Strengthened Forces Along Jordan Border," *Ma'ariv*, December 25, 1990.

41. Michal Yudelman, "Israel will Certainly Retaliate if Saddam Attacks, Levy Says," *Jerusalem Post*, January 9, 1991.
42. "Arens: 'We are Ready and Prepared, and if Attacked we will Respond Without Hesitation,'" *Yediot Aharonot*, January 11, 1991.
43. "The CoS: 'We are Ready for any Contingency,'" *Ma'ariv*, January 13, 1991; David Rudge, "Arens: 'If attacked, Israel will Respond,'" *Jerusalem Post*, January 14, 1991.
44. Bradley Burston, "More Iraqi Missiles May Bring Retaliation," *Jerusalem Post*, January 21, 1991.
45. "Shamir: 'The Distribution of Gas Masks does not Signal Aggressive Intention Toward Iraq,'" *Ha'aretz*, October 8, 1990.
46. "Minister Moshe Arens: 'I am Calm--No Need to Distribute Gas Masks Now,'" *Ma'ariv*, August 10, 1990; Emanuel Rosen, "Where is Israel's Red Line," *Ma'ariv*, August 17, 1990; Akiva Eldar and Eitan Rabin, "Minister Levy Demands Distribution of Gas Masks Without Delay," *Ha'aretz*, August 20, 1990; Eitan Rabin, "Shomron: 'Israel will not Intervene in Military Confrontation in the Gulf,'" *Ha'aretz*, August 26, 1990.
47. Shmaya Kaidar, "Alert Declared in Air Force," *Ma'ariv*, August 12, 1990.
48. Eitan Rabin, "Commander of IAF Bin-Nun: 'No Choice but to get Iraqi Dictator off Stage,'" *Ha'aretz*, September 2, 1990; Eitan Rabin, "Commander of IAF: 'The Force is on High Alert; Pilots Sitting in Aircraft,'" *Ha'aretz*, January 11, 1991.
49. Eitan Rabin, "Three Patriot Batteries to Remain in Israel," *Ha'aretz*, March 3, 1991.
50. See Jill Smolowe, "Turning Up the Heat," *Time*, April 16, 1990.
51. Akiva Eldar *et al.*, "Saddam Hussein: 'If Attacked--We'll Destroy Half of Israel;'" Rabin: 'Let Him not Provoke Us,'" *Ha'aretz*, April 3, 1990; "Rabin: 'Iraq is not Beyond Our Range,'" *Ma'ariv*, April 3, 1990.
52. Dan Margalit, "Rabin: 'For Israel, this is a Deluxe War; the Next Ones will be More Painful,'" *Ha'aretz*, February 19, 1991; Reuven Pedatzur, "Beginning to Emerge from the Basement," *Ha'aretz*, April 3, 1991.

53. See Yair Evron, *Israel's Nuclear Dilemma* (Tel Aviv: Hakibutz Hameuchad, 1987), p. 20
54. "Israel's Retaliatory Capacity is Sharp and Painful," *Ma'ariv*, December 30, 1990 (emphasis added).
55. Ran Dagoni, "Ambassador Shoval: 'The Iraqi Chemical and Biological Threat Must be Eliminated,'" *Ma'ariv*, December 30, 1990.
56. "Israel's Ambassador in Belgium: 'Israel will not Respond with Nuclear Weapons to an Iraqi Chemical Attack,'" *Ha'aretz*, January 1, 1991.
57. See Pedatzur, "Beginning to Emerge from the Basement," *Ha'aretz*, April 3, 1991.
58. Transcript of interview by US Secretary of Defense Richard Cheney, to CNN Pentagon Correspondent Wolf Blitzer on CNN Cable News Network's 'Evans and Novak' program, February 2, 1991. Subsequently, CNN correspondent Blitzer told this author that his impression was that Mr. Cheney had chosen his words very carefully on that occasion, and hence was sending a clear deterrent message.
59. Emanuel Rosen, "Arens: 'Saddam Would Have Reason to Worry if he Uses Chemical Weapons,'" *Ma'ariv*, February 4, 1991; Akiva Eldar, "'Saddam would have Reason to Worry' Says Arens When Asked about Nonconventional Weapons," *Ha'aretz*, February 4, 1991.
60. Akiva Eldar, "Arens: 'Saddam has Crossed the Red Line,'" *Ha'aretz*, January 28, 1991; Shimon Shiffer and Rami Tal, "Saddam Already Crossed the Red Line," *Yediot Aharonot*, January 28, 1991; Bradley Burston and Abraham Rabinovich, "Arens: 'Iraq has Crossed the Red Line,'" *Jerusalem Post*, January 28, 1991.
61. Dani Sade, "The 'Red Line'--The Use of Nonconventional Weapons Against Israel," *Yediot Aharonot*, February 4, 1991.
62. See Shai Feldman, *Israeli Nuclear Deterrence*. See also Ariel Levite and Emily Landau, *Israel's Nuclear Image in Arab Eyes 1960-1991* (Tel Aviv: Jaffee Center for Strategic Studies, forthcoming).

10. Concluding Remarks: Reflections on Deterrence Beyond the Superpower Context

Ariel E. Levite

The rationale underlying the initial symposium, and now this subsequent volume of edited papers, was our desire to explore the relevance for the Middle East of deterrence theory.

Deterrence is by no means a post World War II phenomenon. The application of deterrence strategy dates back to the early days of the creation of the universe and mankind. God then engaged in what we nowadays (following Thomas Schelling[1]) call "deterrence by punishment," admonishing Adam not to eat from the forbidden fruits of the Tree of Wisdom. Since those days, deterrence has been practiced quite frequently, as the title of a classic in the field (*Deterrence Before Hiroshima*[2]) implies. Yet much of the resort to what we presently refer to as deterrence strategy has been unwitting, at times even unconscious. Moreover, deterrence has not always been the principal defining characteristic of interstate relations, let alone the single most important aspect of global world order, that it became between 1945 and 1990.

It is only with the advent of the nuclear age, as Barry Buzan so aptly observes in this volume, that deterrence became not only a common practice, but also a preoccupation of theorists. Yet it is precisely for this reason that so much of the theory of deterrence is grounded in the specific geographical, social, military, and technological (especially nuclear) conditions, as well as the political realities, of the superpower Cold War relationship.

The Middle East context has clearly been marginal to the evolution of deterrence theory. Yet nowhere has the practice of deterrence been so commonplace or its application so prominent as in the Middle East in recent decades. To underscore this observation, it suffices to look at several recent examples, all drawn from the 1990s. In the course of the Second Gulf War, the US and its coalition partners practiced deterrence against Iraq (to dissuade it from invading Saudi Arabia, and from resorting to chemical weapons). Following Saddam's virulent April 2, 1990 speech, Israel practiced deterrence against Iraqi aircraft and missile (and subsequently chemical) attacks, and against Jordan (admitting foreign expeditionary forces on its territory). Also, Turkey and Egypt simultaneously tried to deter Iraq from attacking their territory.

Iraq, in turn, initially actively sought to dissuade Israel from attacking its nuclear assets. It later expanded its effort to cover not only all other Israeli attacks on Iraq, but also any aggression directed at other Arab countries stretching from Mauritania to Syria. It likewise tried to deter the US from launching a military campaign to liberate Kuwait. Iraq-oriented deterrence has continued in the aftermath of the Gulf. Israel has continued to practice deterrence against Iraqi missile attacks, chemical weapons attacks, and Iraqi forces' deployment in Jordan, while the US and the UK have led the UN-coordinated effort to dissuade Iraq from harassing Kuwait and from forcefully repressing its own Kurdish and Shi'ite populations.

Deterrence has been actively pursued during this period elsewhere in the Middle East as well. Israel has been energetically practicing basic deterrence versus Syria, and in another context also against the fundamentalist Muslim terror organization Hizballah in Lebanon. Libya has redoubled its efforts to dissuade the West from launching another attack on its territory or infrastructure, and Iran and Pakistan have repeatedly issued deterrent warnings directed at Israel. In fact, deterrence has played such a salient role in the contemporary Middle East that one of its leading students even conceptually elevated it (mistakenly we submit) to the level of Grand Strategy.[3]

Yet, we cannot help but wonder whether deterrence strategy deserves the central position it presently occupies in Middle East politics. For one thing its regional track record, as far as one can validly judge it empirically, is at best mixed. For another thing, its theoretical underpinnings seem somewhat shaky and context-specific. With these doubts in mind, we embarked on an exercise designed to explore the relevance of deterrence for the Middle East in three successive stages. First, to inquire into the state of the art of theory in this field. Secondly, to explore the link between deterrence theory and practice in other contexts. And finally, to examine the relevance of both for the unique circumstances prevailing in the Middle East. The papers presented at the symposium were purposefully designed to address each of these issues.

What have we emerged with from the symposium?

Our first observation pertains to the state of the theory of deterrence. Much academic work has been devoted to the study of deterrence, especially over the past 20 years.[4] It has produced numerous valuable insights into the dynamics and mechanics associated with deterrence as both a phenomenon and a strategy. As a result, we clearly understand much better many of the intricacies associated with the application of deterrence and key variables that are likely to affect its outcome. Yet the extensive research has made rather limited progress in developing a predictive theory of deterrence, let alone a predictive theory of non-nuclear deterrence (a distinction to which we shall return later). This outcome, however, hardly comes as a surprise to anyone familiar with the difficulties of formulating theory with predictive power for other areas of human conduct.

A related observation has to do with the difficulties and limitations inherent in an inductive approach to developing a theory of deterrence. As George Downs points out, this approach runs into formidable obstacles ranging from the definition of deterrence, via the determination of the universe of cases (where deterrence has actually been attempted), to the analysis and assessment of deterrence success or failure (whether the outcome was determined by the original or manipulated intentions, or by the quality of implementation of deterrence posture). Both Bruce Russet and Yair Evron grapple with these methodological problems in their essays, seeking to overcome them, in part, by introducing the distinction between "general" and "immediate" (or "specific") deterrence. Russet explains how employing the distinction can affect our determination of the universe of cases as well as the assessment of deterrence success or failure. Evron demonstrates the utility of the distinction for evaluating the track record of deterrence in the Arab-Israeli context.

A third observation to have emerged from the symposium, in our mind a critical one, reinforces the importance of the aforementioned distinction between nuclear and non-nuclear (especially conventional) deterrence. Deterrence theory and whatever insights it has to offer for deterrence strategy pertain first and foremost to nuclear weapons. This is not merely a matter of nuclear weapons being in a class by themselves in terms of destructive potential. Other categories of nonconventional weapons, especially biological ones, though clearly inferior in lethality and destructive power, are also so capable of inflicting sufficient casualties as to rightly deserve to be incorporated under the label of weapons of mass destruction (WMD). Even conventional weapons may legitimately be included in that category, and here we mean not only exotic conventional armaments such as fuel-air explosives, but virtually all conventional weapons, assuming that they are applied mercilessly and in abundance.

So the point here is not that nuclear weapons are unique in their overall ability to kill, wound, damage and destroy, or that they are even the most dangerous such weapons, which they undoubtedly are. Rather, it is to emphasize that nuclear weapons are widely acknowledged to have unique inherent qualities as deterrence instruments. The qualities most frequently noted in this regard are the sheer destructive power of even a single such armament, their enduring impact, and their measurable physical impact--deriving, among other things, from the practical inability to defend against them. Consequently, in principle a would-be aggressor is able to calculate ahead of time with sufficient accuracy and certainty the cost to him of a (nuclear) response that he may provoke. This is widely believed to be so grave as to outweigh whatever potential benefits the said would-be aggressor may have hoped to derive from his action, even when the likelihood falls well short of a hundred percent. No other armaments present an obvious combination of these qualities, and they therefore cannot come even close to the deterring power of nuclear weapons.

The widespread perception of the unique advantage of nuclear weapons as instruments of deterrence should not, however, lead one to conclude that they are omnipotent in this regard. Put differently, they might not suffice to deter a determined or desperate[5] aggressor in certain circumstances (especially when considerable doubt exists about the likelihood of nuclear retaliation--see below). No certainty can ever exist that nuclear weapons will attain the hoped for dissuasion effect. Moreover, even when they do seem to work at a given time, there usually remains a persistent anxiety that sooner or later they might fail.

Here we echo another insight that has so vividly emerged from our symposium, namely that uncertainties regarding the efficacy of nuclear deterrence have been commonplace in the post World War II era, both in the superpower context and beyond it. True, the deterrence posture against a Soviet attack on the US mainland had been widely (although by no means universally) considered to be quite sturdy. But profound anxiety whether nuclear deterrence would indeed work has characterized virtually all of its other applications, especially relating to extension of the deterrence umbrella to other regions or scenarios.

Here we have in mind the classical applications of extended deterrence (i.e. Western Europe, Japan, Korea, etc.). But we also refer to other types of efforts to extend deterrence to non-existential threat scenarios. A case in point is Israel's perceived nuclear deterrence. Even its leading proponents tend to discount its efficacy against anything but an Arab threat to the very existence of Israel. That both the Yom Kippur War and the Iraqi missile attacks against Israel happened after Israel was reputed internationally to possess a nuclear weapons capability (including in Arab eyes[6]) seems to lend credence to this belief.

Some of the perennial uncertainty over the efficacy of deterrence has to do with possible deviations from the so-called "rational deterrence model."[7] One school of deterrence theorists ascribes much importance to cognitive deviations from rationality deriving from motivated misperceptions.[8] Others, however, put more emphasis on departures from a rational deterrence relationship grounded in either cultural-normative or political differences existing between the deterring and target countries, as well as in the extreme adversarial relationship prevailing between them. Empirically, the latter are commonly integrated into a discussion of the rationality of the opponent, both instrumentally (the ability to calculate alternatives and choose a preferred course of action on the basis of its cost-effectiveness) and substantively (normative preferences). Such considerations, for example, were a major source of concern for the US even when it was dealing exclusively with the Soviet Union.

Throughout the Cold War doubts persisted whether the Soviet leadership was able to weigh options rationally in view of (a) information constraints, as well as (b) distortions inherent in a totalitarian decisionmaking process. Of even greater concern in this regard was the lingering suspicion that the Soviet Union might be partially or totally insensitive to US deterrence threats of mass destruction given the value system of its leadership, which was colored by cultural gaps, Marxist ideology, and hostile images of the US. Interestingly enough, similar concerns are commonplace in deterrence relationships also outside the superpower context (see below).

Finally, it is worth recalling the inherent fundamental limitation of deterrence, namely that it is not a strategy suited for conflict resolution. As Craig and George put it,[9] the most it can do is to freeze a conflict. Whatever time is thereby gained might better be utilized engaging in creative diplomacy to resolve the conflict, otherwise the deterrence relationship will probably ultimately collapse. Yair Evron reiterates this point in his contribution to this volume when he states that deterrence "is only a management strategy of limited duration." He goes on to emphasize, and later also to illustrate in the context of the Arab-Israel conflict, that although deterrence can be a highly successful strategy, ultimately "when politics are divorced from military deterrence, prospects for the latter's success actually diminish."

The political context may not only undermine a deterrence relationship; it also accounts for an important drawback of deterrence strategy, especially one based on threats of stiff punishment. As Barry Buzan points out earlier in this volume, any deterrence relationship predicated on threats of mass destruction seems to contain an element of self-fulfilling prophecy. Threats of massive retaliation can only be justified and legitimated if the conflict is believed to be an existential one. Yet continued reliance on such threats of retaliation may, in turn, also unfortunately perpetuate the existential conflict.

Deterrence Beyond the Superpower Context

Many of the aforementioned shortcomings of deterrence strategy are exacerbated, and new ones added, once we move beyond the superpower context. Take rationality, for example. Deterrence strategy is often applied by states separated not only by extremely bitter historical rivalry, but also by profound religious, ethnic, and cultural differences, as well as sharply dissimilar political cultures and types of regime. Such a situation largely characterizes the Indo-Pakistani, Greek-Turkish, and Arab-Israeli contexts, to name just a few of the relevant cases.

This divergence generates widespread concern over possible distortions in communication and interpretation of messages between the two rivals, with all their attendant implications for the efficacy of a deterrence posture. Moreover, it raises the ominous prospect of failure of deterrence grounded in the misidentification or mistargeting of assets of "real value" for the would-be aggressor's leadership. As such it gives rise to profound anxiety over the reliability of standard deterrence threats of denial and/or punishment. Here, the lingering anxiety is that these might prove insufficient or even totally irrelevant for purposes of preventing war from erupting (or a conflict from escalating); and, conversely, that they might prove counterproductive, having a self-fulfilling quality, exacerbating tensions and provoking escalation that neither side desires. In his contribution to this volume, Gabriel Ben-Dor echoes such concerns in the Arab-Israeli context, analyzes their roots, and discusses some potential remedies for them.

Concern over the impact of departures from rationality was acute, but not necessarily warranted, in the superpower context. In that case, however, nuclear weapons are widely credited with having ultimately had a stabilizing influence on the relationship.[10] The stabilizing influence of nuclear weapons in this context, in turn, appears to have been a result of the combination of nuclear realities (calculable potential for Armageddon and the inability to defend against them) coupled with the successful socialization over time to nuclear realities. Yet it must be remembered that the virtues of Mutual Assured Destruction (MAD) accorded by nuclear weapons are much more appreciated and extolled in retrospect than they were in real time, when the anxieties inherent in living in a MAD world predominated.

Outside the superpower context, however, the concern that deterrence might be undermined by political, social, or cultural differences is greatly accentuated, not in the least because most conflicts do not have an overt and direct or immediate nuclear dimension. This is to say that calculations necessary to communicate and understand deterrent messages are inherently more complicated given the uncertainties permeating the assessment of the impact of conventional military encounters.

Even in the few cases where nuclear weapons are available to one or more of the adversaries in the Third World (e.g., India and Pakistan), or alleged to be in the possession of such a party (e.g., Israel), they are believed to have only a limited (although, as Shai Feldman demonstrates, by no means negligible) capacity to contain conflict, cool down tempers and stabilize an already existent balance of deterrence in a manner approximating the impact they are credited with having in the superpower context. Indeed, most analysts presently believe that the potential for miscalculation and war in the Third World at least does not diminish, and may actually grow precisely when nuclear weapons are introduced into the equation.[11] This view is attributed, in part, to technical, geographic and resource constraints on fielding survival nuclear forces in this part of the world, and in part to diverse political factors.

Included among the latter are the type of regime and the maturity of the polity. Most disturbing in this context are one or more traits that characterize many regimes in the Third World (unstable, non-democratic or quasi-democratic, non-accountable, ruthless) as well as a political culture that is slow to adjust to the realities associated with the advent of nuclear weapons.[12]

The problems plaguing nuclear deterrence strategy in the Third World are further complicated by the current existence (e.g., PRC, India, and Pakistan) or prospects (e.g., in the Middle East) of more than two nuclear rivals that are neither formally nor practically members of (just) two opposing alliances. The existence or potential emergence of several nuclear states introduces diverse additional complications into the already problematic deterrence equation. These relate to both short-term and long-term stability, predictability and preemption, arms races and prevention. In view of the abovementioned factors, it is commonly argued that even the basic instincts of survival cannot be confidently counted upon to make mutual nuclear deterrence relationships stable and reliable.[13] This conclusion is quite plausible, and the logic underlying it seems quite sound. We must, however, remind ourselves that in retrospect they may nonetheless be proven to have been entirely wrong. At present, despite the lingering doubts and intrusive concerns, there is no valid basis to dismiss such a possibility.

Be the ultimate outcome as it may, it will do little to change one basic fact, namely that the limitations imposed on deterrence strategy, and its shortcomings, are quite profound. The practice of deterrence requires an investment of resources, does not eliminate uncertainty, and hardly guarantees a satisfactory outcome. Furthermore, as Shai Feldman so aptly demonstrates in his contribution to this volume, at times a deterrence posture, especially when it is a credible one, may actually prove counterproductive, whetting the appetite for aggression, rather than diminishing it. Nevertheless, deterrence continues to enjoy broad appeal worldwide among scholars and practitioners alike. Robert Jervis has characterized deterrence theory as "probably the most influential school of thought in the American study of international relations."[14]

But this is not a uniquely contemporary American phenomenon. Take for example Libya's maverick leader Muammar Qaddafi. In explaining the US air attack on Libya in 1986, he pointed out to his people that the entire post World War II global order was predicated on a balance of deterrence. Libya, according to Qaddafi, would not have been attacked in 1986 had it had at the time the capacity to retaliate against New York, a situation he was determined to rectify.[15]

The ubiquity of deterrence in world politics, the Third World included, is neither an aberration nor a transient phenomenon. Nor, we submit, is it grounded in a mythical belief in the omnipotence of deterrence. Robert Jervis suggests that much of the appeal of deterrence theory ought to be credited to its intellectual power, the elegance (and parsimony) of the intellectual framework (coupled with the articulateness of its proponents), the fit between the arguments and the prevailing view of international relations, and the general links between deterrence and realism.[16] These factors by themselves, we submit, cannot explain the appeal of deterrence strategy, as well as theory, to both practitioners and theorists not only in the US but also well beyond it and, intuitively at least, in earlier times as well.

We thus offer additional explanations for the appeal of deterrence. One explanation suggests that deterrence derives much of its popularity from a powerful practical logic--the lackluster alternatives to deterrence available to states and their leaders, especially in eras or contexts characterized by both adversarial relationships and disincentives to the actual use of force. The latter may be grounded in norms proscribing the premeditated use of force and/or in cost/risk matrices driving down its potential utility. The emergence of nuclear weapons has clearly given this last point a new meaning. Either way, Yitzhak Rabin's contribution to this volume vividly illustrates that the attraction to deterrence stems from the unavailability of any superior policy options. Other explanations, which are by no means necessarily mutually exclusive, concern motivations lying partially or completely outside the immediate relationship with the adversary one is supposedly seeking to deter. These point to the need or desire to practice deterrence in order to reassure one's domestic population against the threat, and/or to pressure one's allies/patrons into solidifying their commitment to your security as a manner of dissuading unilateral action on your part.

Irrespective what motivation(s) originally propel a state to adopt a deterrence posture, its efficacy in attaining the desired goal(s) is clearly of paramount importance to both policymakers and analysts. The burden consequently shifts to the consideration of recipes for bolstering the efficacy of deterrence. Prescriptions range from the overt nuclearization of one or more parties to the conflict,[17] to the adoption of discriminate deterrence or decapitation strategies (which is explicit in Gabriel Ben-Dor's recommendations and in Yitzhak Rabin's formulation of the Israeli deterrence posture, both contained in their respective contributions to this volume). Athanassios Platias' paper draws attention to other, more diplomatic avenues for enhancing one's deterrence posture through alliance membership.

By way of conclusion, it ought to be stated clearly that our conference provided no valid basis for assessing the utility of any of the specific remedies proposed for addressing the failings of deterrence. Nevertheless, we are at least able, on the basis of the insights offered by our contributors, to put all of these proposed remedies in perspective. First, since they are all based on our highly imperfect understanding of the deterrence phenomenon, it is only prudent to treat them all with caution combined with a healthy degree of skepticism. Secondly, given that so much of the defense relationship is contextual, even if any of these remedies turns out to be successful in one case, there is no valid basis to infer that it will prove effective in other instances as well. Third, the success or failure of a remedy cannot be determined until after the remedy has been put to the real test. And fourth, even then it may prove impossible to identify with any confidence a given case as a deterrence success or failure, let alone to determine the causes of either.

Notwithstanding the above caveats, the practice of deterrence and the efforts to perfect the strategy of deterrence are likely to continue to occupy both scholars and practitioners, even if the nature of international conflict and the norms governing its resolution continue to undergo a profound change. The tools of deterrence may change over time, but its essence and appeal are not likely to go away so long as the relationship among states, nations, societies, or groups thereof remains a central feature of the international system.

Notes

1. Thomas Schelling, *Arms and Influence* (New Haven: Yale University Press, 1966).
2. George H. Quester, *Deterrence Before Hiroshima: The Airpower Background of Modern Strategy* (New York: J. Wiley, 1966).
3. See Avner Yaniv, *Deterrence Without the Bomb: The Politics of Israeli Strategy* (Lexington, MA: Lexington Books, 1987).
4. Important work on deterrence, especially in the nuclear context, was published between the late 1940s and the early 1960s. Yet the renaissance of the study of deterrence is widely believed to have begun with the appearance of George and Smoke's pioneering systematic study of deterrence. See Alexander George and Richard Smoke, *Deterrence in American Foreign Policy* (New York: Columbia University Press, 1974).
5. Richard Ned Lebow and Janice Gross Stein deserve much credit for having focused our attention on the heretofore little explored phenomenon of the need-driven opponent (as distinguished from the opportunity-driven opponent) and its implications for deterrence. See, for example, *When Does Deterrence Succeed and How Do We Know?* Occasional Paper no. 8 (Canadian Institute for International Peace and Security), February 1990; "Beyond Deterrence," and "Beyond Deterrence: Building Better Theory," in *Journal of Social Issues*, 43:4 (1987), pp. 5-72, 155-170. The beauty and importance of this distinction notwithstanding, it still runs into considerable problems of falsifiability and empirical application.
6. For an extensive discussion of the Arab perception of Israel's nuclear activity and posture see Ariel Levite & Emily Landau, *Israel's Nuclear Image in Arab Eyes 1960-1991* (forthcoming).
7. For extensive background on this debate over rational deterrence theory, it is useful to review the articles in a special issue of *World Politics*, 41:2 (January 1989).
8. See, for example, Lebow and Stein, fn. 5 above.
9. Gordon Craig and Alexander George, *Force and Statecraft*, 2nd Edition (New York: Oxford University Press, 1990), pp. 194-95.

10. See, for example, John Mearsheimer, "Back to the Future: Instability in Europe after the Cold War," *International Security* 15:1 (Summer 1990), pp. 5-56.

11. See, for example, Michael Sturmer; Bo Huldt: Papers Presented at the Second Ginosar Conference on Security and Arms Control in the Middle East, "Confidence Building and Verification: Prospects for the Middle East," January 8-10, 1993 (Jaffee Center for Strategic Studies, Tel Aviv University).

12. An authoritative discussion of the prospects for nuclear exchanges in the event of a new Indo-Pakistani war is provided by Gordon Oehler, the CIA's National Intelligence Officer for Science, Technology, and Proliferation, quoted in an article by Bill Gertz, "India, Pakistan Cited in Spread of Nuclear Arms," *Washington Times*, October 31, 1992. See also: *Senate Governmental Affairs Committee Hearing on Proliferation Threats of the 1990s*, February 24, 1993.

13. See, for example, Lewis A. Dunn, *Containing Nuclear Proliferation*. Adelphi Paper no. 263 (London: Brassey's for the IISS, Winter 1991).

14. Robert Jervis, "Deterrence Theory Revisited," *World Politics*, 31:2 (April 1979), p. 289.

15. Muammar Qaddafi, Tripoli JANA in Arabic, 1115, GMT, June 6, 1991, *FBIS-NES*-91-110, June 7, 1991.

16. Jervis, "Deterrence Theory Revisited," pp. 289-90.

17. See Waltz, "Nuclear Myths;" Shai Feldman, *Israeli Nuclear Deterrence: A Strategy for the 1980s* (New York: Columbia University Press, 1982); Shireen Mazari, "Nuclear Issues: Options for Pakistan," *Strategic Perspectives*, no. 1 (Summer 1991); and Shireen Mazari, "Missile Developments in India and Pakistan and Its Impact on Regional Security," in Gotz Neuneck and Otsfried Ischebeck, eds., *Missile Technologies Proliferation and Concepts for Arms Control* (forthcoming).

Biographical Sketches

Gabriel Ben-Dor	Professor of Political Science and former Rector at the University of Haifa.
Barry Buzan	Professor of International Studies at the University of Warwick; Research Director at the Center for Peace and Conflict Studies at the University of Copenhagen.
George W. Downs	Professor of Political Science at Princeton University, in Department of Politics at Woodrow Wilson School, and at the Center for International Studies.
Yair Evron	Professor of Political Science at Tel Aviv University.
Shai Feldman	Senior Research Associate and Director of the Middle East Arms Control Project at the Jaffee Center for Strategic Studies, Tel Aviv University.
Aharon Klieman	Professor of International Relations and former chairman of the Political Science Department at Tel Aviv University; Senior Research Associate at Jaffee Center for Strategic Studies.
Ariel Levite	Senior Research Associate and Director of Israeli Security Project at the Jaffee Center for Strategic Studies, Tel Aviv University.

Athanassios Platias	Assistant Professor of International Relations at Panteion University; Senior Researcher at the University's Institute for International Relations.
Yitzhak Rabin	Israel's Prime Minister and Defense Minister. Previous positions include: Prime Minister, Defense Minister, IDF Chief of Staff, Israeli Ambassador to the US.
Bruce Russett	Dean Acheson Professor of International Relations and Political Science at Yale University.

The Jaffee Center for Strategic Studies (JCSS)

The Center for Strategic Studies was established at Tel Aviv University at the end of 1977. In 1983 it was named the Jaffee Center for Strategic Studies in honor of Mr. & Mrs. Mel Jaffee. The objective of the Center is to contribute to the expansion of knowledge on strategic subjects and to promote public understanding of and pluralistic thought on matters of national and international security.

The Center relates to the concept of strategy in its broadest meaning, namely, the complex of processes involved in the identification, mobilization and application of resources in peace and war, in order to solidify and strengthen national and international security.

JCSS International Board of Trustees

Chairman: Melvin Jaffee
Immediate Past Chairman: Joseph H. Strelitz (deceased)

The Joseph Alexander Foundation, Ted Arison, Robert H. Arnow, Arnold Y. Aronoff, Newton D. Becker, Jack Berlin, Mr. & Mrs. Harry Blumenthal, Henry Borenstein, Edgar M. Bronfman, Simon Chilewich, Bertram J. Cohn, Stewart M. Colton, Lester Crown, Danielle and Shimon Erem, Allan Fainbarg, Dr. Gerald Falwell, Jacob Feldman, Arnold D. Feuerstein, David Furman, Guilford Glazer, Eugene M. Grant, Vernon Green, Martin J. Gross, Michael M.H. Gross, Irving B. Harris, Betty and Sol Jaffee, Marvin Josephson, Philip M. Klutznick, Judy and Joel Knapp, Fred Kotek, Raymond Kulek, Max L. Kunianski, Mark Lambert, Rose Lederer, William Levine, Morris L. Levinson, Edward C. Levy, Peter A. Magowan, Judd D. Malkin, Stephen Meadow, Hermann Merkin, Milken Family Foundation, Monte MonAster, Max Perlman, Milton J. Petrie, Gary P. Ratner, Raphael Recanati, Meshulam Riklis, Morris Rodman, Elihu Rose, Malcolm M. Rosenberg, Irving Schneider, George Shrut, Marvin Simon, Ruth Sinaiko, James C. Slaughter, Lillian Solomon, Ed Stein, Herb Stein, Walter P. Stern, Dr. Robert J. Stoller (d.), Leonard R. Strelitz, Lawrence A. Tisch, David Warsaw, Jack D. Weiler, Marvin A. Weiss, Emanuel A. Winston, Bert Wolstein, Paul Yanowicz

JCSS Publications

JCSS Publications present the findings and assessments of the Center's research staff. Each paper represents the work of a single investigator or a team. Such teams may also include research fellows who are not members of the Center's staff. Views expressed in the Center's publications are those of the authors and do not necessarily reflect the views of the Center, its trustees, officers, or other staff members or the organizations and individuals that support its research. Thus the publication of a work by JCSS signifies that it is deemed worthy of public consideration but does not imply endorsement of conclusions or recommendations.

Editor
Aharon Yariv

Executive Editor
Joseph Alpher

Editorial Board

Mordechai Abir
Yehezkel Dror
Saul Friedlander
Shlomo Gazit
Mordechai Gur
Yehoshafat Harkabi
Walter Laqueur

Yuval Ne'eman
Yitzhak Rabin
Aryeh Shalev
Israel Tal
Saadia Touval
David Vital

The Jaffee Center for Strategic Studies
Recent Publications in English

1993-1994 Subscription Series
Study no. 21 Aryeh Shalev, *The Israel-Syria Armistice Regime 1949-1955*.
Study no. 22 Aharon Klieman and Ariel Levite, eds., *Deterrence in the Middle East: Where Theory and Practice Converge*.
Study no. 23 Shai Feldman and Ariel Levite, eds., *Arms Control and the New Middle East Security Environment*.
Study no. 24 Aryeh Shalev, *Israel and Syria: Peace and Security on the Golan*.
Study no. 25 Shai Feldman, ed., *Confidence Building and Verification: Prospects in the Middle East*.

The Middle East Military Balance 1993-1994
   Edited by Shlomo Gazit; with Zeev Eytan.

1991-1992 Subscription Series
Study no. 18 Mark A. Heller, *The Dynamics of Soviet Policy in the Middle East: Between Old Thinking and New*.
Study no. 19 Dore Gold, *Israel as an American Non-NATO Ally: Parameters of Defense-Industrial Cooperation*.
Study no. 20 Karen L. Puschel, *US-Israeli Strategic Cooperation in the Post-Cold War Era: An American Perspective*.

War in the Gulf: Implications for Israel
   Report of a JCSS Study Group. Edited by Joseph Alpher.
The Middle East Military Balance 1992-1993
   Edited by Shlomo Gazit; with Zeev Eytan and Amos Gilboa.

Books
Abraham Ben-Zvi, *The United States and Israel: The Limits of the Special Relationship* (New York: Columbia Univ. Press, 1993).